ROOTS OF SCRIPTURE

The Prophetically Influenced Priestly Critique of Human Institutions and Its Relevance for Today

ROOTS OF SCRIPTURE

The Prophetically Influenced Priestly Critique of Human Institutions and Its Relevance for Today

Nicolae Roddy

OCABS PRESS
ST PAUL, MINNESOTA 55124
2024

Roots of Scripture: The Prophetically Influenced Priestly Critique of Human Institutions and Its Relevance for Today

ISBN 1-60191-057-6

Published by OCABS Press, St. Paul, Minnesota.

Books are available through OCABS Press at special discounts for bulk purchases in the United States by academic institutions, churches, and other organizations. For more information please email OCABS Press at press@ocabs.org.

Abbreviations

ABD	*Anchor Bible Dictionary*
ACJS	Annual of the College of Jewish Studies
AJS	*American Journal of Sociology*
AJS Review	Association for Jewish Studies
BAR	*Biblical Archaeology Review*
BZAW	Beihefte zur Zeitschrift für die alttestamentlische Wissenschaft
CBQ	*The Catholic Biblical Quarterly*
CUSAS	Cornell University Studies in Assyriology and Sumerology
IEJ	*Israel Exploration Journal*
IOS	*Israel Oriental Studies*
JBL	*Journal of Biblical Literature*
JHS	*Journal of Hebrew Scriptures*
JPSP	*Journal of Personality and Social Psychology*
JSOT	*Journal for the Study of the Old Testament*
JSOTSup	*Journal for the Study of the Old Testament*, Supplement series
JUE	*Journal of Urban Economics*
LXX	Septuagint
MT	Masoretic Text
OCABS	The Orthodox Center for the Advancement of Biblical Studies
SAOC	Studies in Ancient Oriental Civilization
SBL	Society of Biblical Literature
SHANE	Studies in the History of the Ancient Near East
SJOT	*Scandinavian Journal of the Old Testament*
TROS	*The Rise of Scripture*
VT	*Vetus Testamentum*
VTSup	*Vetus Testamentum*, Supplements
ZAW	*Zeitschrift für die Alttestamentliche Wissenschaft*

Books of the Older Testament

Gen	Genesis	Job	Job	Hab	Habakkuk
Ex	Exodus	Ps	Psalm	Zeph	Zephaniah
Lev	Leviticus	Prov	Proverbs	Hag	Haggai
Num	Numbers	Eccl	Ecclesiastes	Zech	Zechariah
Deut	Deuteronomy	Song	Song of Solomon	Mal	Malachi
Josh	Joshua	Is	Isaiah	Tob	Tobit
Judg	Judges	Jer	Jeremiah	Jdt	Judith
Ruth	Ruth	Lam	Lamentations	Wis	Wisdom
1 Sam	1 Samuel	Ezek	Ezekiel	Sir	Sirach
2 Sam	2 Samuel	Dan	Daniel	Bar	Baruch
1 Kgs	1 Kings	Hos	Hosea	1 Esd	1 Esdras
2 Kgs	2 Kings	Joel	Joel	2 Esd	2 Esdras
1 Chr	1 Chronicles	Am	Amos	1 Macc	1 Maccabees
2 Chr	2 Chronicles	Ob	Obadiah	2 Macc	2 Maccabees
Ezra	Ezra	Jon	Jonah	3 Macc	3 Maccabees
Neh	Nehemiah	Mic	Micah	4 Macc	4 Maccabees
Esth	Esther	Nah	Nahum		

Acknowledgments

About five years into my teaching career—sometime around 2004—I was surprised to receive a phone call from my former Old Testament professor at St. Vladimir's Seminary, Fr. Paul Nadim Tarazi, whom I had not seen in roughly fifteen years. A few weeks later we were having coffee at one of my local midtown Omaha "satellite offices" engaged in a discussion over Scripture and our continuing involvement with it. I discovered I still had a great deal to learn from my teacher whose approach had developed over the years, and I was pleased that he graciously agreed to lecture before two sections of my Sophomore-level Older Testament on the following day.

To those who have heard Fr. Paul speak, it will come as no surprise to learn that my students were mesmerized. Listening to his lecture that morning transported me back to my bewildering days at SVS, when this timid disciple of Fr. John Meyendorff (memory eternal), convinced that St. Maximos Confessor had the answer to every theological problem the West had ever faced, slipped as far down behind my desk as I could to evade the deafening thunderclaps coming from the front of the room. One of them must have popped the bubble of Byzantine theology that surrounded my head, for a little over a decade later, with a Ph.D. in early Jewish and Christian society and literature in hand, I was offered a tenure-track position in Old Testament at Creighton University.

Before Fr. Paul's visit I had been leading my class in a comprehensive exploration of major themes in the Former Prophets that deal with the final days of the Judahite kingdom. I had not mentioned this fact at all, and when Fr. Paul asked me what I thought he should lecture about, I said I would leave it entirely up to him. What happened that morning could be likened to a thousand-piece jigsaw puzzle missing the single piece that would pull the picture all together, which Fr. Paul happened to produce from his pocket. Not only did he nail the topic I had planned to address—the development of which should be apparent by the end of the book—but with far greater erudition, nuance, and poignancy than I could have delivered at that stage in my career. Although Abouna's work has developed even further since those days, it will come as no surprise to those who know him that he left us much to talk about, and his brief stay with my family left me with so much more to consider.

I have since enjoyed several years of warm friendship, collegiality, and inspiration as a member of an international fellowship of pastors, academics, and educated laypersons from many walks of life who follow this consummate teacher in dedicating themselves to "the love, study, and proclamation of Scripture" through the Orthodox Center for the Advancement of Biblical Studies (OCABS). According to its website (www.ocabs.org), the current incarnation of OCABS was established in 2014, following upon the heels of two significant events in the world of Orthodox biblical studies, namely: 1) the falling asleep of His Eminence, Metropolitan Philip, of the Antiochian Archdiocese, "whose love for the God of Scripture occasioned His Eminence's ecclesial blessing for the ongoing work of OCABS"; and 2) Fr. Paul's professional retirement from a distinguished career in the study of Scripture that began in 1970. It is with appreciation for Fr. Paul and his ongoing work—and in solidarity with his past, present, and future students who strive to hear and promote the God of Scripture—that this volume is dedicated. Finally, I am grateful to my wife, Alexandra, and our longtime friends, Andrea Bakas, Fr. Marc Boulos, Fr. Timothy Lowe, and Fr. Bill Mills for their invaluable gifts of time, effort and encouragement that brought this manuscript to its present form.

Nicolae Roddy
Creighton University

Contents

Foreword

Reading *The Roots of Scripture*, Shakespeare's *"Something is rotten in the state of Denmark"* (*Hamlet*, Act 1, Scene 4) comes to mind. But according to Roddy, not only Denmark, but every polity, country or city, around the world cloaks an insidious malady at its center, manifesting itself in dark and dire times for all: terrorism and proxy wars in the Middle East, massive forced relocation of wartime and climate refugees across the globe, fragile economies tottering on collapse, human rights violations of all kinds, not to mention political scandals and sociocultural upheavals at a level never before seen. Yet as Scripture reminds us, we should not be surprised as there is really "nothing new under the sun." (Eccl 1:9).

As Professor of Hebrew Bible/Older Testament at Creighton University for the past quarter century, Roddy is in a position to write such a book. Using idolatry as a paradigm, he highlights the prophetic perspective that timelessly addresses the trouble with all human institution, namely political leadership, cities, weaponry, economic systems, temples, and even the prophetic guild itself. Apparently, Roddy would have us see trouble everywhere. The reader may ask, from whence does this trouble originate? The answer is clearly stated in the Introduction. Roddy writes,

> The ultimate source of the problem is the human ego in its effort to cope with the latent fears and insecurities of everyday life by becoming a kind of god over all. This results in an illusion of control, a lack of faith that invites misguided reliance on the products of human hands in a way that is not only hubristic but idolatrous.

So there you have it! *We* are the source and summit of our world's problems, or as many a mother has said, "You made your bed, now lie down in it." Strong words from mom, strong words from Roddy, strong words from Scripture.

While all of this may seem helpless and hopeless, Roddy reminds us that indeed there is hope; however, this hope lies outside of ourselves. The human condition is so broken, so hurting, so dysfunctional, and disoriented that we cannot fix ourselves, although many have tried. Philosophies failing, we learn that only obedience to the God of Scripture, and not the god of our own invention, sets human beings on wisdom's path. By eschewing ultimately idolatrous reliance on the works of our own hands and taking up Yahweh's steadfast love (*hesed*) for others (including those we may not know or may not like), manifested in the two-sided coin of justice and righteousness (*mishpat ve-zedakah*), we have means for navigating humanity's institutional troubles. For those of you who are shepherds, this preaches!

V. Rev. Fr. William C. Mills
Pascha 2024

Introduction

This book explores the process of biblical formation in a way that highlights the diverse tapestry of traditions and interests, forms and genres that underlie the forging of the scriptural message between the Babylonian exilic period and into the Hellenistic period.[1] Despite politicizing emendations to the text added during the period from Ezra-Nehemiah and through the Hasmoneans,[2] the scriptural message is predicted on the conviction that the hearing of scripture is not only supremely edifying for authentic living, but crucial for addressing the precarious ills human beings have wrought upon themselves. But why examine the process involved in the *formation* of scripture and not just focus on the finished product, especially since many of us have often heard Fr. Paul Tarazi refer to the use of traditional historical methodologies, including archaeology, as a "slap in the face of God"? First, as an archaeologist and historian I understand these words to be a dramatic critique of the way these methodologies have been exploited for vain religious and scholarly agendas and not so much a condemnation of the sciences themselves. After all, critical methodologies, like all technologies, are merely tools employed by a user for an end, a process that must be honest, objective, and above all true to the text. Second, my twenty-five-year plus career in archaeology, historical research, and teaching has not hindered me at all in the task of imparting to students what I take to be the crux of the Bible's scriptural message, which can be condensed into the simple dictum "I Am," thus you are not. Last, but not exhaustively, I am convinced the roots of scripture germinate in the real-world experience of a sixth-century BCE nation whose history had

---

[1] As such, the present study serves as prologue to Fr. Paul Nadim Tarazi's magisterial *The Rise of Scripture* (St. Paul, MN: OCABS Press, 2017), hereafter, *TROS*.

[2] For more on Hasmonean politicization, see Philip Davies, "The Hebrew Canon and the Origins of Judaism, pp. 194–206 in *The Historian and the Bible: Essays in Honour of Lester L. Grabbe*, edited by Philip R. Davies and Diana V. Edelman (New York: Bloomsbury, 2011).

come to a full stop with the destruction of its political and religious institutions—human-made constructs that in retrospect failed to deliver upon their promises and protections. Similarly, because humanity continues to invest heavily in monumental superficiality and impermanence, a closer look at the prophetic perspective seems a worthwhile endeavor.

The question here is whether an intertextual study of the process of formation leading to the production of the Bible can be enlisted in service to the scriptural message by clearing away popular presuppositions and assumptions about its relationship vis-à-vis actual history and geography.[3] Obviously, I am convinced it can. This critical approach to the process of biblical formation is intended to illumine the path toward its crowning apotheosis as scripture, a modest bridge bringing the educated parishioner equipped with the ability and desire to think critically to connect the world that produced the Bible with the world of today in light of the timeless message of scripture as expounded in such works as *TROS* and OCABS's various *Bible as Literature* and Ephesus School podcasts.[4]

Any detailed account of how the Bible came to be can only be hypothetical and is certainly less important than hearing it as Scripture. This book is aimed at educated non-specialists who might be interested in both history and Scripture by viewing the world we inhabit through the lens of the biblical prophets.[5] To draw the contrast, prudent use of the tools of traditional critical methodologies can be helpful and should appeal to Orthodox clergy, scholars, and laymen alike who are not intimidated by

---

[3] By Bible as Bible I mean the emergence into history of a loose collection of selected and edited oral and textual materials, replete with dissonant voices expressed through a variety of genres, and generally cohering into a grand narrative of a people's re-envisioned, pre-exilic past.

[4] Marc Boulos and Richard Benton, hosts. *Bible as Literature* podcast. Ephesus School, https://ephesusschool.org.

[5] For further reading on what prophetic literature has to say to today's society, see Walter Brueggemann's classic, *The Prophetic Imagination* (40th anniversary edition, Minneapolis, MN: Fortress Press, 2018) and Abraham Heschel's timeless work *The Prophets* (New York: Harper & Row, 1962, reprinted 2001).

bold scientific inquiry. It is a commonplace that the Church interprets the Older Testament through the lens of the New Testament as interpreted by the chorus of early Fathers; however, as Orthodox Christians I would also hope we can affirm the Older Testament has having a voice of its own without which the New Testament would be unintelligible.[6] One should also remember that the Fathers were less exegetes than homileticists, focused as they were on passages interpreted as foretelling the coming of Christ[7] and leaving today's expositors to grapple with the bulk of what remains using the modern tools at hand. I think the apprehension many Orthodox Christians experience in subjecting the sacred text and tradition to critical scrutiny lies in not knowing what to do with the results. But if one really believes that the Bible is "true" (in ways other than being historically or geographically so), there should be no hesitancy in examining it more closely.

The present work asserts that rigorously applied critical methodologies can be marshaled in service to the Older Testament, and therefore to the Gospel, by focusing especially on the prophetic critique of human institutions, which (among other things) foreshadows such things as Christ's pronouncement against the Jerusalem temple that "not one stone will be left upon another; all will be thrown down" (Matt 24:2) or "rendering unto Caesar the things that are Caesar's and to God the things that are God's" (Mk 12:17 / Matt 22:21). The prophets shatter the illusion of security and well-being that arises from the casual, often unconscious investment of trust in the works of our hands, understood as a form of idolatry. This

---

[6] The New Testament quotes the Older Testament hundreds of times, ranging from nodding allusions to the Greek scriptures to full quotations, sometimes even with the source cited (e.g., Lk 3:4).

[7] Those interested in further research should consult *The Ancient Christian Commentary on Scripture* series (ACCS), ed. T. C. Oden (Westmont, IL: InterVarsity Press), or Eerdman Publishing's Church's Bible series, ed. Robert Louis Wilken (Grand Rapids: Eerdmans Publishing). Additionally, John Willis's topically-organized *The Teachings of the Church Fathers* (San Francisco: Ignatius Press, 2004) may also be of interest.

broader application of idolatry is rooted in the foremost command of having "no gods before me" (Exod 20:3; Deut 5:7), which underlies Jesus's pronouncement, "You cannot serve God and wealth" (Matt 6:24; Lk 16:13), or Paul's identification of greed as idolatry (Col 3:5).

The prophetic perspective not only launched the Bible's eventual reception as sacred scripture for the pre-modern world but provides relevance for addressing today's secular world as well. How so? Anyone who takes time to read prophetic literature closely and carefully discovers a worldwide playing field leveled and cleared, a primordial wilderness wiped clear of prideful human achievements—our endless succession of Babels—exposing the fact that standing naked before God, no one is privileged.[8] The ultimate source of the problem is the human ego, which endeavors to become a kind of god over all in its effort to cope with the latent fears and insecurities of modern life. The result is an illusion of control, a lack of faith that invites misguided reliance on the products of human hands in a way that is not only hubristic but idolatrous. One could argue that setting oneself up as a god (or as God) is the fundamental human predicament, illustrated in the story of the expulsion from Eden (Gen 3:5),[9] or the interruption of the tower of Babel's construction (Gen 11:1-9).

Selected Relevant Scholarship

Those who have kept up with the field of biblical studies over the past half-century may wonder how this project fits in the flux of the so-called minimalist-maximalist debate. Modern

---

[8] Rabbi Saul of Tarsus, aka the Apostle Paul, understood the Hebrew scriptures in writing that God shows no partiality (Rom 2:11) and that "all have sinned and fall short of the glory of God (Rom 3:23).

[9] The serpent's words, "You shall be as God [or gods]," spoken to Eve, who "saw the tree was good for food and to be desired to make one wise," are not untrue, for the only thing that distinguishes gods from humans in the ancient world is that the former have special knowledge and live forever. Thus, the humans and their descendants are denied access to the tree of life by the cherubim who guards the way with a flaming sword (Gen 3:24).

discussions over the historicity of the Hebrew Bible / Old Testament began in the early 1970s, at which time the field of biblical studies was shaken by the publication of critical studies that seriously challenged the historicity of its texts. These seminal works, most notably Thomas Thompson's *The Historicity of the Patriarchal Narratives* and John Van Seeters' *Abraham in History and Tradition*, launched an academic movement, led most notably by the Copenhagen and Sheffield schoolsea,[10] which resulted in the organization of full-blown academic program units in European and American professional society meetings throughout the 1990s that are still going strong today.[11]

Over the years, the critical methodologies of the so-called minimalists eroded the historicity of the patriarchs and matriarchs and went on to be applied to other foundational narratives of "ancient Israel,"[12] namely the Exodus story and the conquest accounts of Joshua and Judges. More recently and into today, the biblical portrayal of the grand and glorious kingdom of David and Solomon, which traditional scholarship dates to the early tenth century BCE, continues to be the subject of vigorous debate in light of these new literary and historical critical methodologies, especially archaeology (although applied

---

[10] Thomas L. Thompson, *The Historicity of the Patriarchal Narratives* (BZAW 133; Berlin: de Gruyter, 1974); John Van Seeters, *Abraham in History and Tradition* (New Haven: Yale University Press, 1975). Other seminal works include Neils Peter Lemche, *Early Israel: Anthropological and Historical Studies on the Israelite Society Before the* Monarchy (VTSup 37; Leiden: E. J. Brill, 1985); Philip Davies, *In Search of "Ancient Israel"* (JSOTSup 148; Sheffield: JSOT Press, 1992); and Thomas L. Thompson, *Early History of the Israelite People from the Written and Archaeological Sources* (SHANE 4; Leiden: Brill, 1992). Lemche joined with Thompson as founders of the Copenhagen school, while Davies and his students represent the Sheffield school. These schools are regarded as the premier centers of biblical "minimalism."

[11] See the excellent collection of essays in Lester Grabbe, ed., *Can a History of Israel Be Written?* (JSOTSup 245; Sheffield: Sheffield Academic Press, 1997).

[12] The expression "Ancient Israel" is a variable scholarly construct that refers to the obscure community that produced the Bible.

mostly by non-archaeologists).[13] The furthest limit of the debate is perhaps represented by scholars like Niels Peter Lemche of the University of Copenhagen, who argues the entire Older Testament to be a thoroughly Hellenized work, merely acknowledging the possibility that "general historical recollections from an earlier period" may be embedded within it.[14]

The present volume does not involve itself in the minimalist-maximalist debate except to observe how the polemic suffers from mischaracterizations and misrepresentations coming from both sides. Minimalists do not generally deny a process of formation in which some historical artifacts survive in biblical texts: neither are all maximalists biblical literalists or shoddy, misled historians. The shifting playing field at the nexus of scholarly skepticism has been a hot topic in popular "biblical archaeology" venues like *Biblical Archaeology Review*, founded in 1975, which at times has appeared to exploit polarization for the sake of sales among its largely conservative Christian readership.[15] It especially continues ubiquitously *ad nauseum* on YouTube, mostly from biblical conservatives on the defense over "biblical inerrancy" issues. For this reason, I prefer to avoid labels and permit archaeological data and biblical texts to speak for themselves, leaving it to the reader to see where they

---

[13] One notable exception is archaeologist Israel Finkelstein, professor emeritus at Tel Aviv University and long-time director of excavations at Tel Megiddo. See Israel Finkelstein and Neil Asher Silberman, *The Bible Unearthed: Archaeology's New Vision of Ancient Israel and the Origin of Its Sacred Texts* (New York: Touchstone, 2002).

[14] Niels Peter Lemche, *The Israelites in History and Tradition* (Louisville, KY: Westminster John Knox Press, 1998 (p. 182), cited in Marc Brettler, "The Copenhagen School: The Methodological Issues," *AJS Review* 27:1 (2003): 1-22 (5-6); see also Niels Peter Lemche, "The Old Testament—a Hellenistic Book?" SJOT 7 (1993): 163-93, as well as his latest monograph, *The Old Testament Between Theology and History: A Critical Survey* (Westminster John Knox Press, 2008).

[15] *Bible Archaeology Review* is the magazine of the Biblical Archaeology Society, a non-sectarian organization founded by Herschel Shanks in 1974. To its credit, in the early 1990s, BAS was instrumental in opening the Dead Sea Scrolls to wider scholarly access. In 2018, Shanks, formerly an attorney, was succeeded by Robert Cargill, a reputable biblical scholar and archaeologist, who I trust will moderate BAR's longstanding sensationalism.

may or may not connect. At any rate, it is possible to see why the maximalist position has continued to lose ground over the years.

Another movement arose in the 1970s that also involved a departure from the oft-dry excesses of the historical-critical method, albeit for other reasons. Introduced by Brevard Childs' in *Biblical Theology in Crisis* (1970) and developed further in his *Introduction to the Old Testament as Scripture* (1979), the method popularly known as canon criticism came to focus on the final form of biblical texts and their implications for communities of faith.[16] Canon critics have no problem accepting the general findings of modern biblical scholarship, but their interests remain largely theological, less so historical, reading the text as living scripture.[17] The question arises over whether one can truly appreciate the hearing of scripture without some consideration of its constituent materials, processes, and influences.

While the present work nods in affirmation of scripture's final form taking shape during the third and second centuries BCE, it seems oddly impractical to ignore the process of biblical formation leading up to it—something akin to throwing out the proverbial baby with the bathwater. Even if inspired scripture were to fall full blown from heaven, components of the Bible certainly did not. Clearly, the Bible is not monolithic. Biblical minimalists and canon critical scholars appear willing to acknowledge that some portions of the Bible were written before—perhaps even well before—its final revision during the Hellenistic period.[18] To assert the Bible is a purely Hellenized book, or that the shape of the canon had no formative process

---

[16] Brevard Childs, *Introduction to the Old Testament as Scripture* (Philadelphia: Fortress Press, 1979); Mark G. Brett, *Biblical Criticism in Crisis? The Impact of the Canonical Approach on Old Testament Studies* (Cambridge: Cambridge University Press, 1991); Rolf Rendtorff, *Canon and Theology* (Minneapolis: Fortress Press, 1993).

[17] Childs, *Introduction*, 82-83.

[18] For a critique of some of the basic arguments put forth by Thompson and Lemche, see Brettler, "Copenhagen School."

is to ignore the preponderance of material and literary evidence to the contrary, much of which will be covered here. Can the raw materials that contributed to the rise of scripture be seen behind latter stages of canon formation that result in the Bible as scripture? This book argues for the affirmative. It explores how a community of prophetically influenced priestly scribes attempted to grapple with certain ultimate questions arising from real events, specifically the sixth-century BCE destruction of Jerusalem's palace-temple complex, and how their efforts helped provide the raw materials that would create a self-critical literary past.[19] Therefore, as a point of departure we begin with the (neo-)Babylonian conquest of the Levant, a historical event strongly evidenced by widespread destruction levels in the material record of the southern Levant in the early sixth century BCE.

It is all but certain that the Bible as *Bible*—that is, the self-critical aspect this book explores—came together in response to the destruction of Jerusalem's palace-temple complex.[20] This is not to say that earlier oral and written traditions did not exist, only that it took a cataclysmic event—namely, the demise of the nation—to evoke a concerted scribal effort to make sense of it all. The literary enterprise that resulted in the formation of the Bible would pave the way to navigating the political and cultural challenges of the Persian and Hellenistic periods, resulting in its acceptance as enduring scripture, not some mere literary artifact.[21] To be sure, it is not always possible to determine at which point in the process a particular word or idea may have been introduced or edited to meet some new situation; however, the increased use of Aramaic vocabulary and spellings of certain

---

[19] See Tarazi, *The Rise of Scripture* (St. Paul, MN: OCABS Press, 2017), which advances the thesis that scripture emerges as a self-deprecating take-down of the Hellenistic polis and everything associated with it.

[20] Excavations overlooking the Kidron valley in east Jerusalem south of the Temple Mount witness to a sixth-century BCE destruction, although its full extent is not known.

[21] It is important to realize that this is only the beginning of a process of canon formation yet to culminate in the fullness of Bible as scripture.

names—for example, Jegar-Sahadutha in Gen. 31:47[22]—indicates revisions continued being made into the Persian and Hellenistic periods. Likewise, the Deuteronomistic history largely retains names and terms as found in Assyrian and Babylonian cuneiform tablets from the seventh and sixth centuries BCE. The spelling of Hezekiah in 2 Kings, for example, agrees with Assyrian cuneiform sources from the late eighth-century BCE, such as Sennacherib's prism, but appears contemporized as Yizekiah in the Chronicler's account and the Dead Sea Scrolls.[23] These and other examples thus evidence a process of formation leading up to the final form of these texts.

The Bible as Bible: The Road toward Scripture

Traditionally, the Torah (also known as the Pentateuch, or the Five Books of Moses) has been regarded as a kind of lemma for the entire Bible, most likely since its promulgation by the priestly scribe Ezra in fifth-century BCE Jerusalem. According to the book of Ezra, the post-exilic community heard an iteration of the Mosaic law, which was strictly interpreted to the point of shunning other peoples of the land (*am ha-aretz*) to the point of expelling priests' wives and children who had not been among the returnees from Babylon (Ezra 10:11; Neh 10:30). This is not the place to critique Ezra's policies regarding his strict and selective application of the Torah; however, distancing the rigors of the law from the prophetic principles of justice (*mishpat*) and righteousness (*tzedakah*)—that is, the Law from the Prophets—appears to have set the stage for subsequent generations of both Jews and Christians to repeat many of the same mistakes that led to Jerusalem's destruction and exile in the first place. In sum, the Priestly law stipulates what must be done to remain holy in proximity to the tabernacle, while Deuteronomy and the Prophets show how to attain and retain

---

[22] "Laban called it Jegar-sahadutha [Aramaic: "heap of ruins"], but Jacob called it Galeed [Heb: "heap of ruins"]."

[23] Brettler, "Copenhagen School," 11-12.

holiness through steadfast love (*hesed*) for God and others, manifested in action through the twinned attributes of justice and righteousness (*mishpat ve-zedakah*, to be described in greater detail elsewhere).[24]

Recent literary critical studies, mostly European, suggest that the inaugural form of the Bible did not begin with the Torah, or Pentateuch, but as a corpus of nine books—an Enneateuch, if you will, comprising some form of the books of Genesis through 2 Kings.[25] The roots of this paradigm can be traced to the schools of two renowned twentieth-century German biblical scholars, Gerhard von Rad (1901–1971) and Martin Noth (1902–1968), both of whom had devoted their professional lives to identifying the relationships among the Hebrew Bible's constituent literary forms and sources. On the one hand, von Rad established the textual and thematic continuity between the books of Deuteronomy and Joshua, leading him to posit a corpus known as the Hexateuch, while Noth on the other hand demonstrated how the book of Deuteronomy functions as a literary and thematic prologue to the Former Prophets (Joshua through 2 Kings), which led him to posit a Deuteronomistic history (*Überlieferungsgeschichte*),[26] or Dtr in scholarly shorthand. Thus, the book of Deuteronomy provides the theoretical keystone that unites both scholarly paradigms in serving as both the culmination of the Torah and the prologue to Prophet corpus. This suggests that someone—most likely the priestly scribe Ezra—appropriated the five scrolls of the Torah for a

---

[24] See Philip P. Jenson, *Graded Holiness: A Key to the Priestly Conception of the World* (Sheffield, UK: Sheffield Academic Press, 1992).

[25] See Thomas B. Dozeman, T. Römer, and K. Schmid, *Pentateuch, Hexateuch, or Enneateuch?: Identifying Literary Works in Genesis through Kings* (Atlanta: Society of Biblical Literature, 2011). If one is dealing in terms of scrolls, the number would be eleven—technically, an undecateuh—given that 1 and 2 Samuel and 1 and 2 Kings add up to four scrolls. Incidentally, although the book of Ruth is technically numbered among the Writings (Ketuvim), it appears between the books of Judges and Samuel in most Christian canons because its setting seems to fit a pre-monarchic setting.

[26] Martin Noth, *Überlieferungsgeschichte des Pentateuch* (Stuttgart: Kohlhammer, 1948), reprinted as *A History of Pentateuchal Traditions* (Englewood Cliffs, NJ: Prentice-Hall, 1972).

strictly theocratic agenda while isolating them from the Prophets, a practice that continued throughout the life of the party of the Sadducees. It can be argued that by structurally and ideologically distancing the five scrolls of the Torah from the prophetic corpus, the self-corrective mediation offered through prophetic concepts like steadfast love (*hesed*), justice (*mishpat*), and *righteousness* (*tzedakah*) would be lost along with a fuller understanding of what it might mean to be created in the image and likeness of God (Gen 1:26-27). Is it possible that such liberal Deuteronomistic principles stood in the way of Ezra's strict and exclusionary holiness agenda?

It was Noth's assertion that Dtr was compiled in the aftermath of the destruction of Jerusalem based on the fact that it is the last major event it covers and that it is bolstered by the many prophecies *ex eventu* purporting to "foretell" the event scattered throughout the work.[27] Roughly two decades later, in 1968, Harvard professor Frank M. Cross advanced the view that Dtr had been written in two stages; namely, that it was originally a triumphalist work composed during the reign of king Josiah in the latter half of the seventh century BCE (Dtr[1]), but was overhauled a few decades later to become a scathing self-assessment of what had gone so terribly wrong that Yahweh would destroy his eternal city and house (Dtr[2]).[28] A number of studies have appeared since that show the picture to be far more complicated than this; however, the idea of a general two-phase process survives.

---

[27] A prophecy *ex eventu*, also known as *vaticinium ex eventu*, is a literary device in which an event that has already occurred in the writer's past is presented in the form of a prophecy, such as the interpolation of Solomon's second dream (1 Kgs 9:1-6; 2 Chr. 7:12-22) or the foretelling of the seventh century BCE king Josiah inserted into the narrative world of the tenth-century BCE (1 Kgs. 13:1-2).

[28] Frank. M. Cross, "The Structure of the Deuteronomistic History," in *Perspectives in Jewish Learning*, edited by J. M. Rosenthal, 9-24. ACJS 3 (Chicago: College of Jewish Studies, 1968). The material also appeared in Cross's *Canaanite Myth and Hebrew Epic: Essays in the History of the Religion of Israel* (Cambridge: Harvard University Press, 1973), 274–89.

Evidence for this two-stage literary process is most obvious in the stories of Israel's kings, where earlier materials favorable to the monarchies of Israel and Judah appear to have been retained to illustrate just how far their kings could fall. Israel's first monarch, Saul, for example, is introduced as tall and handsome (1 Sam. 9:2) and a valiant warrior (11:5-11); however, the Lord soon "regrets that he made Saul king" (15:10-11), whereupon the king tragically spirals into a kind of paranoid schizophrenia (16:14-15) and ends up taking his own life (31:4). Similarly, Saul's successor, David, is introduced as a popular young hero who tends his family's sheep, composes soothing music (1 Sam.16:14-23), and slays lions and Philistines by his own hand (1 Sam. 17:43-50); yet this same David manages to shatter practically all ten commandments in forty-eight hours (2 Samuel 11). In doing as he wishes because he can, David in effect sets himself up as a god before God, and when one breaks this preeminent commandment ("You shall have no other gods before me, Exod 20:3), the rest soon fall like dominoes. Lastly, but not exhaustively, the Lord appears to Solomon in a dream and grants him wisdom to rule wisely (1 Kgs 3:5-14); however, one finds only a single explicit example of wise counsel (see 1 Kgs 3:16-28). The fact he marries a thousand wives who lead him into idolatry (1 Kgs 11:1-3) would seem to call his godly wisdom into question. These dichotomous portraits retain aspects of the sort of triumphalist pro-monarchical descriptions one expects to find in royal archives, perhaps like those lost chronicles mentioned frequently throughout the Deuteronomistic history, namely, the *Annals of the Kings of Israel* and the *Annals of the Kings of Judah*. As we will see in Chapter Two, Dtr[2]'s last word on Israel's leaders is that they are failed receptacles of trust, wholly unable to deliver the protection expected of them by their misguided flocks.

In the chapters ahead, we will see that the negative critique of the Israelite monarchy is similarly applied in critical judgments against Israel's reliance on fortified cities, chariots of war, the political economy, cultic worship, and even the prophetic guild itself. What do all these things have in common? All are human constructs, "works of the hands" that prove to be little more than illusory repositories of trust squandered for the failed purpose of relieving fear and anxiety in uncertain times. Looking back at the glowing embers of a destroyed Jerusalem— the very city the Lord had delivered from the Assyrians "for the sake of my servant David" little more than a century earlier (2 Kgs 19:34)—the inevitable question arises over why Judah's national deity would permit his city and house to be destroyed. The uncanny, prophetically influenced answer to "What went wrong?" was "We did," an uncanny self-examination that eventually comes to underlie the scriptural enterprise by implicating itself along with every other nation and empire under the judgment of God.

The following chapters guide the reader through relevant biblical texts that highlight the prophetically influenced scribal perspective on failed human institutions, with implications that are as relevant today as they were when their enterprise was first inaugurated. Structurally, each chapter begins with a brief introduction; it then moves to historical, real-world considerations, followed by the prophetical perspective on the topic. Juxtaposing the prophetic perspective with history and the material record exposes the biblical story as being up to something other than providing a reliable historical or geographical record.[29] Because a large portion of the Bible presents stories of the past, most readers accept it as reliably historical and read it as such. As Enlightenment philosopher Baruch "Benedict" Spinoza (1632-1677) observed, people presented with reasonable and coherent statements often believe them at once to be factually true, a view supported by the miasma of half-baked conspiracy theories abounding on

---

[29] Whether one believes the Bible to be an accurate remembrance of geographical places and historical events as they played out or a fictional story woven entirely *ex nihilo*, there is sufficient textual and material evidence to show both positions to be erroneous, with grave implications for Palestinian society and culture today.

social media platforms today.[30] One must be suspicious and self-aware of this human tendency if one is to hear the message of scripture. The question is how the act of writing *ultimate history*—by which I mean the attribution of supernatural causation to real or imagined events of the past—functions to establish a narrative world one experiences as somehow "true." These experiences and the convictions they produce have nothing to do with the material remains of architecture or artifact, save that traces of them are occasionally found embedded in biblical narrative like insects in amber. Nevertheless, significant textual and material remains that provide the raw materials and building blocks for the eventual rise of scripture exist and these will be considered in this work only for purposes of illustrating the contrast between real and narrative worlds.

In sum, it seems to make sense to explore scripture's raw materials and building blocks evident in the diversity of the Bible's various forms and genres that arose out of the profound trauma of Judahite history having come to a full stop. The destruction of Jerusalem in the sixth century BCE and subsequent mass deportations to Babylon are sufficiently attested in the material record. As an archaeologist, I have personally examined the charred remains of a sizeable conflagration stretching over East Jerusalem's sixth-century BCE level, and have viewed images of cuneiform tablets, such as the al-Yahudu tablets, attesting to Yahwistic theophoric names and exilic life gathered from settlements in Babylon;[31] however, none of the following chapters depend on accepting

---

[30] Spinoza's position contradicted Descartes (1596-1650), who asserted that people have the ability to suspend belief about the veracity of something until they have had a chance to assess new information; however, Spinoza's view has been tested and affirmed by at least one recent scientific study; see D. T. Gilbert, R. W. Tafarodi, and P. S. Malone, "You Can't Not Believe Everything You Read," *JPSP* 65.2 (1993): 221-33. For more of Spinoza's views, see B. Spinoza, The Ethics and Selected Letters (ed. S. Feldman; trans. S. Shirley; Indianapolis, IN: Hackett, 1982).

[31] Laurie E. Pearce and Cornelia Wunsch, *Documents of Judean Exiles and West Semites in Babylonia in the Collection of David Sofer* (Ann Arbor, Eisenbrauns, 2014).

the historicity of this or any other biblical event. It is reasonable to imagine that such a catastrophic event (imagine the 9/11 catastrophe multiplied ten times over) would provide a catalyst for thinking about ultimate matters. One could well imagine that exposure to widespread death, destruction, and deportation would conjure up a perfect storm for a community of intelligent, literate sages and scribes to reflect upon their orientation in a perilous world. Judah's cultural and political cataclysm provided inspiration for saying what needed to be said, namely that the Word of God is not an artifact of history but a living voice from the whirlwind barreling down the corridor of generations—the enduring voice of the God of scripture that demands obedience and carries vital implications for living authentically in any era.

As mentioned, each of the following chapters explores the prophetic critique of some Israelite human institution or achievement, namely, the monarchy, the fortified city, military defenses, the political economy, the temple cult and its priesthood, and even the prophetic guild itself. Although an attempt has been made to examine each topic distinctly within its own essay, the reader will see the impossibility of addressing one subject apart from mentioning them all. Case in point, kingship and priesthood co-arise with the fortified city and its temple, resulting in a particular social, political, and economic system that requires a robust supply of chariots and horses and infantry to defend. What all these have in common is the prophetically influenced priestly scribal critique that arose from the smoldering aftermath of Jerusalem's destruction—that by placing ultimate trust in the works of one's hands—idolatry, in other words—Israel had forgotten the Lord God who brought it up from slavery in the land of Egypt and bound its people in obedient servitude to himself. With hindsight as foresight, the prophets assert that the supreme defense provided by obedience to the laws and decrees of the divine King and Shepherd, voiced through the lips of God's fiery chariots and watchtowers—the prophets—had been ignored. In sum, national fear and insecurity in the age of fearsome empires led to misplaced trust in the works of human hands, the most insidious form of idolatry. Might the prophetic perspective have something relevant to say about what it means to be human today, especially in the face of the impending climate catastrophe?

The Prophets and the Climate Crisis

One final word: As a father of five and soon-to-be grandfather, I am convinced that any scholarship that fails to acknowledge the inexorable reality of anthropogenic catastrophic climate change amounts to little more than Qohelethian *hevel*, a vain and worthless endeavor. One recent peer-reviewed journal article by well-established climate scientists asserts:

> We declare, with more than 11,000 scientist signatories from around the world, clearly and unequivocally that planet Earth is facing a climate emergency ... The climate crisis has arrived and is accelerating faster than most scientists expected. It is more severe than anticipated, threatening natural ecosystems and the fate of humanity.[32]

At this writing, long-term steadily rising temperatures are broiling Europe and North America at levels seen never before, a problem the vast majority of scientists contribute to human causation.[33] According to the UN Refugee Agency, climate-related disasters are the cause of more than half of known population displacements in 2022, and that nearly sixty percent of displaced persons now live in countries most vulnerable to climate change.[34] Meanwhile, corporations and states

---

[32] William J Ripple, Christopher Wolf, Thomas M Newsome, Phoebe Barnard, William R Moomaw, "World Scientists' Warning of a Climate Emergency," *BioScience* 70, no. 1 (2020): 8-12, https://doi.org/10.1093/biosci/biz088

[33] Jeff Goodell, *The Heat will Kill you First: Life and Death on a Scorched Planet* (New York: Little, Brown, and Co., 2023).

[34] UNHCR, https://www.unhcr.org/us/news/stories/climate-change-and-displacement-myths-and-facts. Accessed Jan 25, 2024.

committed to the production of non-renewable fossil fuels to meet the exorbitant energy demands of industrialized nations continue to release carbon and other greenhouse gases (GHGs) into the atmosphere, soon passing a point of no return. These toxic gases blanket the planet, trapping its heat and bringing about a demonstrable annual increase in the number of adverse and catastrophic weather events. More importantly, it threatens the overall climate stability of the Holocene epoch, which many geo-scientists assert is being replaced by the Anthropocene, a new geological era named for the global impact humans are having on the earth's environment and bio-systems. Neither energy producers nor their thirsty high-end consumers are likely to alter their disastrous economic symbiosis any time soon; however, an even greater sin against life on planet Earth is the grave injustice done to the world's poor, whose net contribution to the global problem is hardly negligible yet have little means for protecting themselves from a sweltering planet. While most works on the Bible and climate change focus on the creation narratives and psalms for promoting human responsibility in caring for the environment, prophetic literature is decidedly pessimistic in its assertion of humanity's inability to heed warnings to avert its own demise, a human proclivity that in Amos's time led him to proclaim, "For three transgressions and for four, I will not revoke the punishment!"[35]

This book makes no real contribution to the struggle against anthropogenic degradation of the environment apart from calling attention to its looming threat to human life amid the earth's biodiversity, but if indeed the Hebrew Bible arose out of monumental collapse, it is all but certain the post-destruction prophetic perspective that forged a convincing response to what had gone so terribly wrong might have some relevance for

---

[35] See David Wallace-Wells, *The Uninhabitable Earth: Life After Warming* (New York: Penguin Random House, 2019).

today.[36] Despite radically different worldviews between the theistic ancients and us secularized moderns, the shared reality of a looming catastrophe not everyone believed would occur—brought about by the failure of human beings to do what must be done to avert it—suggests it might be helpful to explore prophetic literature's post-destruction diagnosis to see what if anything might be of value in preparing ourselves for navigating the consequences of an impending threat in our own day, regardless of whatever degree or form it may take.

Finally, if the Syrian wilderness lies in the background of the entire scriptural story, as Tarazi asserts—a place where the Shepherd's voice leads the sheep from oasis to oasis in a land devoid of cities and other artificial "works of the hands"—then perhaps the yet unknown outcome of catastrophic climate change may offer a major societal re-set—a fresh start for the planet and surviving species. In any case, without a significant attenuation of human pride and arrogance, naively trusting in "works of the hands" as a guarantee of safety and well-being remains a foolish strategy history repeatedly shows to fail.

---

[36] I am indebted to my colleague, Ronald A. Simkins, for bringing this connection to my attention. Those interested in biblical religion and the climate crisis should obtain a copy of his *Creation & Ecology* (Eugene, OR: Cascade, 2020), which provides a thorough analysis of their intersection.

Chapter 1
Idolatry as Paradigm

You shall not make for yourself a graven image, nor any kind of likeness of anything that is in the skies above, or that is on the earth below, or that is in the water beneath the earth. (Exod 20:3)

He fashions the rest into a god and bows down this, his idol, and worships it; he prays to it and says, "Save me, for you are my god!" (Isa 44:17)

It is a commonplace that the Bible explicitly condemns idolatry, narrowly construed as the worship of other gods through the veneration of representative images (*peselim*) fashioned by human hands in wood, stone, or metal:

> You shall have no other gods before me. You shall not make for yourself any graven image, neither in the likeness of anything that is in the skies above, nor upon the earth below, nor in the waters beneath the earth. You shall not bow down to them nor serve them, for I, the Lord your God am a jealous God, visiting the iniquity of the fathers upon the children to the third and fourth generation of those who despise me. (Exod 20:3-5 // Deut 5:7-9; see also Lev 26:1).

The penalty for transgressing this command is also unequivocal: "He that sacrifices to other gods besides the Lord shall be utterly destroyed" (Exod 22:20). Anyone discovered in the act of worshiping foreign gods, including the sun, moon, or other celestial phenomena shall, on the testimony of two or more witnesses, be brought to the city gate and pelted with stones until dead, that "evil may be purged from your midst" (Deut 17:2-7).

The powerful and frequent warnings against venerating objects dedicated to other gods indicates its pervasiveness in the biblical writers' cultural milieu.[1] The fashioning of objects for religious purposes is a universal human phenomenon that had existed from prehistoric times.[2] Roughly 12,000 years ago, the invention of agriculture in the Neolithic (New Stone) period, led to the development of religious technology believed to ensure seasonable weather, protection from floods, the promise of bountiful harvests, and safe passage to the netherworld. These rituals co-arose with enduringly powerful stories of how everything came to be and how best to survive in a world fraught with dangers all around. In Bronze Age Canaan (ca. 3300–1200 BCE), a plethora of localized gods were known, most of which were subsumed under the chief deities of the region, known as El, Anath, and Ba'al. Other formidable deities included Mot, the god of death. For the Phoenicians, who lived along the coast, Yam, the god of the sea, was prominent. Gods of fertility, agriculture, and war, along with natural phenomena like the sun, storm, moon, and stars were represented by portable figurines kept in the home or accessed through public shrines and temples.[3] Not long after the turn of the Iron Age (ca. 1200 BCE), in the northern hill country of Canaan, priests and prophets devoted to the worship of Yahweh, a relative newcomer to the region,[4] competed with autochthonous fertility

---

[1] See Mark S. Smith, *The Early History of God: Yahweh and the Other Deities in Ancient Israel* (Grand Rapids, MI: Eerdmans, 2002). For shorter articles, see André Lemaire, "Who or What Was Yahweh's Asherah?" BAR 10.6 (1984): 42–51, and Ephraim Stern, "Pagan Yahwism: The Folk Religion of Ancient Israel," BAR 27.3 (2001): 21–29.

[2] The art and artifacts of paleolithic cave dwellers suggest attempts to manipulate or appease the powers of nature for attaining a sense of safety and well-being in the world, including good health, protection from malevolence powers, successful hunts, and so on. See Gregory J. Wightman, *The Origins of Religion in the Paleolithic* (Lanham, Maryland: Rowman & Littlefield, 2014). For a critique of traditional scholarship on the subject, see Ina Wunn, "Beginning of Religion." *Numen* 47, 4 (2000): 417–52.

[3] Notable examples include Bronze Age temples at Arad, Hazor, and Megiddo, which can be visited on the *Virtual World Project*, available at www.virtualworldproject.org.

4 There is no shred of extra-biblical evidence that the Exodus as recounted in the Bible ever occurred. However, it is likely that a core group of Semitic priestly migrants had something of an experience in Egypt that would account for their remembrance of a foundation narrative rooted in slavery and a leader named Moses, a known Egyptian name. Reasoning from demographics, it seems most likely that

cults of Canaan, co-opting the name of the chief god El and subsuming all other gods under its pluralized form, Elohim.[5]

The primary motivation for honoring one god over another rests on a collective hope of deriving the greatest boons and benefits for survival, including rainfall for food security, abundant harvests, and deliverance from hostile forces.[6] Biblical Israel's need for rain during a time of prolonged drought underlies the prophet Elijah's Las Vegas-type extravaganza in pitting Yahweh against the Phoenician Queen Jezebel's patron deity Baal, god of the storm (1 Kgs 18:17-40). Here the prophet chides the Israelites, asking "How long will you pass back and forth [*pasach*] between two opinions? If the Lord is God, follow him, but if Baal, then follow him." (v. 21). The dire need for rain also underlies Hosea's oracle against Yahweh's adulterous wife, who in the shadow of approaching Assyrian conquest chased after Canaanite fertility deities without realizing that Yahweh fulfills all her survival needs (Hos 2:10). Although the biblical text argues that God-above-nature trumps Canaan's gods of nature, it is not difficult to understand how people then and now can so easily default to the security of something solid and at-hand out of vulnerability and fear in an unpredictable and perilous world. Such is the reason for having convenient portable gods like the *teraphim* Rachel steals from her father Laban (Gen 31:32-35), so plentiful in the material record. We

---

this group, the tribe of Levi, migrated into Canaan and set about organizing its burgeoning agricultural population around a single God, whom they called Yahweh, supported by the fact the tribe of Levi receives no tribal designation of their own but dwells in villages throughout the tribal confederacy.

[5] Monotheism developed much later than people suppose. Likely developing as a response to the apparent victory of Marduk, supreme god of the conquering Babylonians, over Yahweh, something Yahwistic priests were unwilling to accept. The worldview that exclusively worships one god without denying the existence of other nations' gods is more appropriately termed henotheism or monolatry, terms distinguished from polytheism that do not disregard the legitimacy of foreign gods.

[6] Orthodox Christians make similar petitions during the Divine Liturgy, "For favorable weather, an abundance of the fruits of the earth, and temperate seasons, let us pray to the Lord . . . For deliverance from all affliction, wrath, danger, and distress, let us pray to the Lord."

want our gods to be close at hand to alleviate our fears and insecurities and feelings of vulnerability. When the God of Scripture seems all too far away, people manage to come up with a new one, as a poem by Romanian poet Nichita Stănescu (1933–1983) observes (my translation):

> Second Elegy, the Getic, to Vasile Pârvan
>
> In every crevice they placed a god.
>
> If a stone split open, they quickly brought
> a god and placed it there.
>
> When a bridge collapsed it was enough
> to set up a god in the empty space.
>
> Or, along the avenue, a hole appears
> in the asphalt where a god may be seated.
>
> O, do not lacerate your hand or foot,
> whether accidentally or on purpose.
>
> For at once they will place a god in the wound,
> as here and there and everywhere,
> they will place there a god
> that we may worship it, because it
> defends everything that is alienated from itself.
>
> Take care, warrior, not to lose an eye,
> because they will bring a god and
> stick it in the socket
> and it will stand there petrified, and our
> souls will stir in praising it,
> and you will betray even your own soul,
> praising it like strangers.

With human concerns for safety and survival at stake, it is easier for most people to trust in one's own devices than stand boldly and mindfully open before ultimate reality—however one imagines it to be. Expecting security and well-being from amulets, talismans, and household gods may be comforting, but placing faith and trust in larger idols—narcissistic demagogues, heartless megacities, overstocked armaments, and magnificent cathedrals—is exceedingly more foolish, and more dangerous. Prophetic condemnation of the idolatrous artisans and the perilous inefficacy of their products can be applied to the illusory measures one might take up today for feeling safe and secure in the world:

> Those who make idols are nothing [*tohu*],
> and what they delight in does not profit [. . .].
> The ironsmith fashions a tool and works it with hammers;
> forging it with his strong arm.
> Indeed, he is hungry and his strength fails,
> He drinks no water and is faint [. . .]
> He kindles a fire and bakes bread,
> then he makes a god and worships it.
> He makes a carved image and bows down before it.
> Half of it he burns in the fire;
> over this half he roasts meat, eats it, and is satisfied.
> He also warms himself and says, "I am warmed by the fire!"
> The rest of it he makes into a god, his idol.
> He bows down to it and worships it; he prays to it and says,
> "Save me, for you are my god!" (Isa 44:9-17; cf. Isa 40:18-20).

The insidious nature of idolatry is such that it lurks imperceptibly in our attitudes toward things we believe will provide safety and security in a world—a world poisoned by unrelenting carbon emissions, ravaged by burgeoning wealth inequality, and imperiled by stockpiles of nuclear weapons vast enough to destroy all life on earth several times over. Idolatry is not something that resides within the things we trust to distract us or deliver us from danger, but a subtle and perilous attitude conjured up within ourselves to subconsciously placate ourselves. Consider the irony that many Americans feel the need to purchase an assault-style weapon in order to feel safe from crime or government, all the while ignoring the epidemic of mass-shootings that mow down innocent children in schools and shopping malls.[7]

Calling out the illogical and illusory nature of everyday reliance on things believed to offer ultimate security is the primary purpose of this book. The trouble with this or that— the subject of each chapter—highlights the propensity for succumbing to illusions about each. The plan throughout the book is to examine each subject in its real-world historical context, then shift to the contrasting prophetical critique of it in a way that demonstrates the relevance of Scripture for today. This paradigm relies on an expanded notion of idolatry defined as trust in something that is believed to offer ultimate safety and security but ultimately does not, demonstrating misplaced trust in the works of our collective hands that distracts us from living authentically in the searing face of the scriptural God.

Idolatry as "Forgetting the Lord"

According to the prophetic perspective, the fundamental human predicament can be framed in terms of Israel's reliance on its own flawed institutions in place of humbling itself in obedience to the Word of God. Motivated by a belief born of fear that it could achieve safety and security in the perilous world of voracious empires, Israel supported strong leaders who turned out to be self-serving, built cities whose walls could not stand, forged weapons that melted before their enemies, erected shrines that God would abandon and destroy, amassed resources that would not be shared with the poor and needy, and heeded prophets who told them what they wanted to hear. These human institutions and endeavors proved to be of no avail for delivering the nation and its people from the ruinous consequences of the misplaced trust they placed in them. Because idolatry is commonly associated with placing trust in

---

[7] A mass-shooting is defined as an incident in which four or more victims are shot or killed. According to the Gun Violence Archive, the US is averaging nearly two mass-shootings per day (www.gunviolencearchive.org),

human-wrought objects associated with religion, it is easy to expand the notion of idolatry to other forms of "works of the hands." One must peer beyond the veil of self-delusion to view the prophetic reality that sees beyond the fleeting distractions of impermanent things. For the prophetically influenced priestly scribes who were able to peer through the smoke and ashes of their devastated city, palace, and temple, it was made clear that ultimate security and permanence rests only in the refining fire of an everlasting God of Scripture. Israel had placed confidence in its own artificial constructs for security and well-being, which turned out to be a futile and foolish endeavor, for the assurances these works promise are but *hevel*—empty, illusory, and fleeting.

The book of Deuteronomy is an effective starting point for understanding the danger of idolatry. This book is not only the fifth scroll of the Torah, or Pentateuch, but serves as prologue to the six books that follow, namely Joshua, Judges, 1 and 2 Samuel, and 1 and 2 Kings.[8] Thus, the book of Deuteronomy provides the link between the Law and the Prophets, offers an iteration of the Torah couched in a series of speeches attributed to the quintessential prophet Moses.[9] In its final chapters, Moses stands overlooking the broad expanse of Canaan from atop the hills of Moab, chiding his flock for their never ceasing complaints and insecurities, and extolling the necessity of obedience to Yahweh's commands and stipulations (*huqqim ve-mishpatim*) upon which their continued survival depends. Just as he had herded his father-in-law Jethro's sheep in the hills of Midian, Moses now "goads" (*lamad*) his human flock with words of warning as they prepare to acquire tenancy of the land before them.[10] Recalling and reinforcing the exhortation given at Sinai and elsewhere along the way (Exod 20:4-5; cf. Exod 20:23;

---

[8] The book of Ruth belongs within the Writings section of the Bible (Ketuvim), but some canons place it after the book of Judges due to its narrative setting.

[9] The three sermons are 1:6–4:40; 4:44–11:32; and 12:1–33:29

[10] See Paul Nadim Tarazi, *Land and Covenant* (St. Paul, MN: OCABS Press, 2009).

34:17; Lev 19:4; 26:1; Deut 4:15–19, 25; 5:8), Moses gives voice
to a dire prophecy *ex eventu*:

> And the generation to come, your children who will arise after
> you, and the foreigner that comes from a far-off land, shall say
> when they see the plagues of that land and the diseases which the
> Lord has brought upon it—and the whole land burning with
> sulfur and salt, nothing sown, nothing growing, nor any
> vegetation, like the destruction of Sodom and Gomorrah, Admah
> and Zeboiim, which the Lord destroyed in his anger and his
> wrath. And all the nations will say, "Why has the Lord done this
> to this land? What was the cause of this hot anger?" Then men
> will say, "It is because they abandoned the covenant of the Lord,
> the God of their ancestors, which he made with them when he
> brought them out of the land of Egypt. And they went and served
> other gods, worshiping them, gods whom they had not known
> and whom he had not permitted them. Thus, the anger of the
> Lord was kindled against that land, bringing on it every curse
> written in this book. The Lord uprooted them from their land in
> anger and in wrath and with great indignation cast them into
> another land, as it is this day." The secret things belong to the
> Lord our God, but the things that are revealed belong to us and
> to our children forever, that we my do all the words of this law.
> (Deut 29: 21-28)

It should come as no surprise that Moses's farewell
admonition, written from a sixth-century BCE perspective with
Assyrian and Babylonian conquests and deportations in the
background, is not so much about entering the land as it is about
remaining upon it—as well as why they did not:

> When you have children and grandchildren and have been long
> in the land, and you act corruptly and make a graven image [*pesel*]
> in any form, thus doing what is evil in the sight of the Lord your
> God to provoke him, I call heaven and earth to witness against
> you this day that you will soon utterly perish from the land that
> you are about to cross the Jordan to occupy. You will not live
> upon it for long but will be utterly destroyed. And the Lord will
> scatter you among the nations; only a few of you will be left
> among the nations into which the Lord will drive you away.
> (Deut 4:25-27)

The wrath of the Lord over the manufacture and veneration of idols (*peselim*) *in any form* (*temunah qol*) is not limited to religious considerations only but can also be applied to Israel's misdirected efforts to find safety, security, and prosperity through the works of their hands. The illusory sense of well-being that results from placing one's faith and trust in human institutions and endeavors instead of in the God of Scripture is simply a more insidious form of idolatry.

According to the book of Deuteronomy, the primary reason for the catastrophe that befell Samaria and Jerusalem was that all Israel had forgotten (*shakach*) the Lord their God, "who had brought them out of the land of Egypt," a fact evidenced by many current and *ex eventu* warnings strewn throughout the book of Deuteronomy (4:9, 23; 6:12; 8:11, 14, 19; see also 2 Kgs 17:38).[11] Because remembering the Lord is tied to the special relationship rooted in Israel's deliverance from bondage, forgetting the Lord means failing to obey the stipulations of the Torah, whether knowledgably or through indifference.[12] Maintaining the covenantal relationship with the Deity by ensuring national ritual purity and upholding moral and ethical principles, especially justice, is key for ensuring the nation's survival; however, Israel at no time learned to walk "in the ways of the Lord" (Deut 10:12, 26:17, 28:9; Jos 22:5; 1 Kgs 3:14, 6:12; 11:38) and therefore was justifiably expelled: "So Judah went into exile out of its land" (2 Kgs 25:21b).

Forgetting the Lord also results in careless foregoing of the benefits and protections expected of a divine patron. The post-exilic revision (Dtr[2]) of the Deuteronomistic history issues a stern *ex eventu* warning against the Israelites exalting themselves in pride over their own accomplishments and good fortune:

---

[11] Prophecy *ex eventu*, or *vaticinium ex eventu*, is a literary device in which an event from the author's past is inserted into the narrative past to appear as having been foretold.
[12] Remembering God (*dhikr Allah*, in Arabic) is also a fundamental principle in the Qur'an.

Take care that you do not forget the Lord your God by not keeping his commandments, his ordinances, and his statutes which I am commanding you today. When you have eaten your fill and have built fine houses and live in them, and when your herds and flocks have increased and your silver and gold is multiplied, be sure not to exalt yourself, forgetting the Lord your God who brought you out of the land of Egypt, out of the house of slavery, and who led you through the great and terrible wilderness [. . .] Do not say to yourself, "My power and the might of my own hand have gotten me this wealth." But remember the Lord your God, for it is he who gives you power to get wealth, so that he may establish the covenant he swore to your ancestors, as he is doing this day. And it shall be that if you do forget the Lord your God and walk after other gods to serve and worship them, I solemnly warn you this day that you shall surely perish. Like the nations that the Lord is destroying before you, so you shall perish, because you would not hearken to the voice of the Lord your God. (Deut 8:11-14, 17-20)

A later sermon in the wilderness foretells the fate of the idolatrous nation, who placed its trust in the works of human hands—an idolatrous people fittingly banished to idolatrous foreign lands:

The Lord will scatter you among all peoples, from one end of the earth to the other, and there you shall serve other gods, of wood and stone, which neither you nor your fathers have known. Among those nations you shall find no repose, no resting place for the sole of your foot; but there the Lord will give you a trembling heart, failing eyes, and a sluggish spirit. Your life shall hang in doubt before you, and you shall fear both night and day, with no assurance of your life. (Deut 28:64-66)

Another prophetic *ex eventu* warning is embedded in Solomon's second dream vision following completion of the temple:

If you turn aside from following me, you or your children, and do not keep my commandments and my statutes that I have set before you, but go and serve other gods and worship them, then I will cut Israel off from the land that I have given them; and the house that I have consecrated for my name I will banish from my sight; and Israel will become a lesson and a taunt among all peoples. This house will become a heap of ruins; everyone passing by it will be astonished, and will hiss, and they will say, 'Why has the Lord done such a thing to this land and to this house?' Then they will say, 'Because they have forsaken the Lord their God, who brought their ancestors out of the land of Egypt, and embraced other gods, worshipping them and serving them; therefore, the Lord has brought this disaster upon them.'" (1 Kgs 9:6-9)

As is commonplace, it is clear that the fundamental human predicament is idolatry, specifically expressed in terms of "forgetting the Lord," which can apply to the naïve investment of trust in human constructs intended to serve as bulwarks against fear and insecurity, religious or otherwise. These works of human hands include:

- the establishment of the monarchy, instead of obedience to the heavenly King (see especially 1 Sam 8:7);

- building fortified cities, instead of trusting in the true refuge (see Psalm 46, which inspired Martin Luther's well-known hymn, "A Mighty Fortress is Our God."

- iron chariots, in place of God's "chariots of fire and horses of fire," that is, the Prophets as Israel's highest and best line of defense;

- the political economy, perverted at the expense of true justice and righteousness on behalf of the poor and needy;

- The temple, despite Jeremiah's warning that God no longer dwells there (see Jer 7:4);

- the prophetic guild itself, which portrays its members as fallible mortals who proclaim the infallible and unfailing word of God.

Conclusion

The prophetic perspective insists that Israel's investment in false repositories of trust resulted in the destruction of Samaria and Jerusalem and brought their national histories to an end. While the Bible asserts that biblical disasters are the result of God's righteous judgment, one does not have to be a theist to accept the reality of widespread mortal transience in the face of human-caused catastrophic phenomena such as nuclear war or adverse climate change. It is hope that our foray into the prophetically influenced priestly critique of human institutions will invite serious thinking about our relationship to the monumental structures and achievements of our own day, all of which carry empty promises of security and deliverance. To what extent can we view these things in their true light—that is, as Scripture does—fleeting, inadequate, and preventing us from standing unafraid in the face of annihilation from the searing gaze of the God of Scripture (Exod 33:20).

Is it even possible to imagine a world where persons walked uprightly, courageously eschewing reliance on divisive and charismatic political demagogues, financial districts, nuclear stockpiles, assault-style weapons, and ornate gargantuan cathedrals? How can reliance on these things deliver what they promise alongside our obvious inability to make the world truly a safer, greener, and more equitable place? There seems to be no end to the manufacture and accumulation of ever more dangerous weapons, daring advancements in AI technology and bioscience that may evade our control, or excessive reliance on non-renewable energy sources leading us to a global catastrophe?[13] A recent Heritage Foundation headline provides a good example of the perilous disconnect between the problem and possible solutions: "The World Is Becoming Ever More Dangerous: The President Must Revitalize the U.S. Strategic Arsenal."[14]

The prophetic perspective affirms the stark reality that people are generally uninterested in changing course to any significant degree, let alone repenting of the evils they foist on fellow humans or on the environment. Remaining on a steady course with no positive earthly end in sight, warnings from ancient and present-day prophets to change direction go unheeded. In many cases, it is already too late to turn back. But what if the end turns out to be the solution? For the only thing one can change for sure is one's attitude toward the seemingly inevitable. In the meantime, we can continue the struggle for prophetic justice and righteousness (*mishpat ve-tzedakah*) within our own communities, with the knowledge that the prophetic hope for a solution may not be one we want to hear: "For three transgressions and for four, I will not revoke the punishment" (Amos 2:6).

---

[13] As of this writing, the largest energy producers, so-called Big Oil (Exxon Mobil, BP, Shell, TotalEnergies and Chevron), are boasting over 200 billion dollars in annual profits for 2022 and increasing annually even as people around the world struggle to pay for heat and electricity. ExonMobil alone disclosed a profit of $59.2 billion, more than double its earnings for the previous year. While the war in Ukraine has affected oil prices, the problem lies in the obscene profits, much of which goes to stock buybacks and shareholder investments.

[14] Written by Robert Peters and Ryan Tully, available at https://www.heritage.org/defense/report/the-world-becoming-ever-more-dangerous-the-president-must-revitalize-the-us (March 1, 2024).

Chapter 2
The Trouble with Kings

The Lord said to Samuel, "Listen to the voice of the people in all that they say to you, for they have not rejected you, but they have rejected me from being king over them." (1 Sam 8:7)

And on that day you will cry out because of the king you have chosen for yourselves, but the Lord will not answer you on that day." (1 Sam 8:16)

The prophetic perspective on Israel's kings offers a reliable model for a critique of leadership in any age. One could argue that the political institutions of hoary antiquity have little in common with today's more complex forms of government; however, because the health of any polity depends on the ability of its leaders to subordinate personal whims and desires to the needs of their constituency, the prophetic critique is timeless, applicable to anyone holding a position of responsibility over the wellbeing of others. Scripture scoffs at the achievements of the mightiest kings and emperors, exposing all their moral failings to the light of day in a way most ancient scribes would hesitate to do lest they be put to death. Instead of engaging in the usual and customary scribal aggrandizement of kings, which their positions and lives depended, prophetically influenced priestly scribes advanced the notion that the Israelite monarchy had been a lamentable idea from the start, and that the violent end of Israel and Judah can be attributed largely to kings, especially Jeroboam and Manasseh respectively (2 Kgs 17:21-23; 23:26-27). Writing sometime after these kingdoms' demise, the scribes revised earlier materials to boldly reveal the inability of kings to fulfill the expectations of their office and consigned the ends of their lives to utter failure. In heightened contrast to grandiose royal chronicles recovered from the dust and sand of the ancient Near East, the scriptural portrait of Israel's kings lays bare human leadership for how it truly is.

Stepping back to view the larger picture, however, we see the dismal portrayal of Israel's kings as merely a foil for a far more serious problem, namely the misplaced trust their subjects invest in them. From the inception of the biblical monarchy, which is naively predicated on the foolish desire to "be like other nations" (1 Sam 8:5), Israel and Judah endure a long line of deplorable monarchs, of which the most popularly celebrated appear to behave most despicably, David, for example. It is ironic that the Israelite elders' desire for a king who would "go out and fight our battles" (1 Sam 8:20) foreshadows the fact that "at the time of year when the kings [of other nations] are leading their armies into battle, David remains in Jerusalem" (2 Sam 11:1). It is clear from the perspective of the prophetic writer that Israel's kings are unable to attain the duty and honor of their counterparts among the nations (despite the fact that victories they win are attributed to Yahweh). In remaining behind in Jerusalem, David takes the opportunity to commit a series of grievous sins—at the very least coveting his neighbor's wife, committing adultery, and orchestrating murder of a loyal warrior. How is it this valiant young shepherd boy whom the Lord had chosen to be king would abandon his human flock to pursue such devious, self-serving ends? Yet David is not the only king to receive such scathing critique. How does Saul go from being a valiant tall and handsome warrior to a paranoid schizophrenic and suicide; or Solomon, the epitome of wisdom, becoming an idolator and a despot? From first to last, the kings of Israel and Judah not only fail to deliver the security and justice expected of them but bring the destructive wrath of God upon themselves and all the subjects which had placed their trust in them.

Kingship in the Ancient Near East

Monarchy, the form of leadership in which unlimited power is wielded by king (less often a queen)[1] is historically the oldest form of government. Its seed germinates from a long-ago era when men capable of getting others to do their bidding were able to overcome challenges to their own power and authority for as long as they could hold on to it, ideally long enough to pass it on to an heir of his choosing. In untroubled times, it was enough to be the respected elder of an extended family, clan, or tribe; but threatening conditions required stronger, more strategic leaders—warrior chieftains, perhaps, who could effectively protect the clan or tribe and its resources from both internal and external challenges. Such were the Judges of the Bible. Depending on the magnitude of the threat, it was sometimes necessary for warrior chieftains to forge pacts with neighboring chieftains that shared common security interests. For this there would be additional costs and risks; for as Samuel, the last of the Judges, warns the Israelite elders, there are serious investments to be made in maintaining a centralization of power (1 Sam 8:10-18). And then there is the matter of diminished status among weaker leaders of any coalition. As such, these consolidations of power were seldom permanent for there would be no need or desire to continue sharing authority once the danger had passed.[2]

Sumerian cuneiform texts of the early Bronze age (late-fourth millennium BCE) recount the rise of kings in Mesopotamia. They begin by witnessing to the pastoral and nomadic tribes that migrated all over region's expansive fertile grasslands unencumbered by the need for social diversification. Some migrating populations began to discover the processes of

---

[1] Notable female rulers include the Sumerian Kubaba of Kish, Egyptian rulers Sobekneferu and Hatsheput, as well as the biblical Athaliah, daughter of Ahab and Jezebel (2 Kgs 11:1-3).
[2] Perhaps one of the best modern analogies is Afghan society, whose tribal chieftains join forces in the face of imperialist threats (Byzantine, Ottoman, Russian, and American) and dissolve their alliances once the invaders have withdrawn.

agriculture early on, about 10,000–12,000 years ago, and began settling down on the fertile plains along rivers and tributaries and near foothills where rain run-off could be pooled in stone-lined dug-out pits. The earliest settlements were usually concentrically arranged and architecturally homogenous, with residential and public buildings differing only in size, an arrangement suggesting centralized, perhaps charismatic leadership emanating outward in governance of personal and community resources.[3] With greater urban development, a division of labor was required for managing efficient food production and distribution; water resource management; construction of homes, public buildings, and defensive structures; tool making; and the management of shrines, temples, and rituals to house and appease local protective deities.[4] With social diversification cones the need for overseers, and sitting atop the social pyramid was the *lugal* (literally, "great man") of the community.

The *lugal* was supported by a cadre of men and women set apart by dint of their special connection with gods and spirits. Diviners, seers, and healers had always played an important role in early societies but became an essential part of the division of labor required by the complexities of settled life for the order they could bring to it. To be sure, knowledge of the sacred and the ritual technology for handling it was serious business, not unlike electricians who must respect the potent energy they are trained to manage. Thus, the priestly class played a supporting leadership role by legitimizing the strong man's power and authority. Albeit rarely, they could question and effectively challenge him as well. Case in point, the northern Levitical priestly tradition reveals its disdain for the institution of

---

[3] A few of these Neolithic settlements can be visited virtually on our Virtual World Project (www.virtualworldproject.org). The concentric subterranean arrangement of the Pre-Pottery Neolithic A period is especially visible at 'Ain Abu Nukhayla, in Jordan's Wadi Rum.
[4] It is interesting that according to early Assyrian inscriptions, the first king, Tudiya, and those who followed him, were known as "kings who lived in tents," suggesting a more pastoral, less urban community.

monarchy in 1 Samuel 8, which accounts for the decommissioning of the Levitical priesthood by King Jeroboam in 1 Kings 12. Over time, the symbiosis of royal and priestly powers came to be evidenced by elaborate architectural styles conjoining palace and temple, imposing edifices often set atop a natural or artificial hill. These impressive structures strengthened the strong man's power over the city-state, legitimizing his rule through an adoptive relationship with its patron deity.[5]

The divine power that legitimized the rule of the *lugal* is evidenced by ancient documents like the *Sumerian King List*. With a few notable exceptions, Mesopotamian rulers were regarded as adopted sons of gods at coronation,[6] a practice reflected in Ps 2:7: "I will tell of the decree of the Lord: He said to me, "You are my son; today I have begotten you." By contrast, Egyptian kings of the Old Kingdom (mid-third millennium BCE), builders of the great pyramids, were often celebrated as true divinities.[7] In any case, laws are enforced by kings empowered by the gods to mediate cosmic laws upon the earth. Ur-Nammu, the late-third millennium BCE founder of the Sumerian Third Dynasty, for example, not only constructed a magnificent ziggurat for the moon god, Nanna-Sin, but also promulgated

---

[5] A historical example of what happens when there is a disconnect between king and priesthood underlies Cyrus the Great's triumphal march into Babylon in 539 BCE, facilitated by the fact that Nabonidus, the last of the neo-Babylonian rulers, had apparently gone mad, abandoned the city for a decade, and returned with zeal to promote his Assyrian mother's moon god, Sin, which he apparently preferred over the Babylonians' chief deity, Marduk. Incidentally, Daniel 4 imputes Nabonidus's insanity to his predecessor, Nebuchadnezzar II, who had conquered Jerusalem. See Paul-Alain Beaulieu, *The Reign of Nabonidus, King of Babylon*: 556-539 BC (Yale University Press, 1989).

[6] There are a few cases in which kings refer to themselves as gods, most notably Naram-Sin of Akkad (latter third millennium BCE), and Shulgi, second king of the Third Dynasty of Ur (end of the third millennium BCE).

[7] By the early second millennium (Middle Kingdom) immortality in Egypt becomes dependent upon a "weighing" of the moral substance of souls, and less an inherent divinity reserved for rulers. See David O'Connor and David P. Silverman, eds., *Ancient Egyptian Kingship* (Leiden: Brill, 1995); Jan Assmann, *Death and Salvation in Ancient Egypt*; translated by David Lorton. (Ithaca, NY: Cornell University Press, 2014).

one of civilization's earliest recorded law codes, no doubt with the expectation that society would submit to the orderly governance of the cosmos.[8]

These forms and aspects of Sumerian civilization—religion, architecture, law and so on—continued in the Akkadian and Old Babylonian periods and up to the Iron Age, at which time a people called "Israel" emerges into the light of history.[9] These arbitrarily labeled ages, designated by historians as Late Bronze and Early Iron, are characterized by the onslaught of fearless kings, who encouraged and empowered by the will of their respective gods developed strategies for wider conquest. For the Assyrians of the Iron Age, this included setting fire to the gates of foreign cities, relocating elite societies, and installing foreign overlords from afar, thus ruling by confusion in the disconnect between language, religion, and custom. The neo-Babylonian (Chaldean) empire followed suit but maintained something of a scorched-earth policy along with the deportation of foreign elites to Babylon.[10] For the unfortunate kingdom of Judah, this included the priest Ezekiel in 597 BCE, followed by King Jehoichin and the Queen Mother roughly a decade later.

It is difficult to imagine what went through the minds of kings and emperors who led their armies westward across the Euphrates River to the Mediterranean Sea and southward toward Egypt. We are fortunate that their scribes left records of

---

[8] Great books on Mesopotamian culture are somewhat dated but remain relevant. These include Samuel Noah Kramer, *The Sumerians: Their History, Culture, and Character* (Chicago: University of Chicago Press, 1971); A. Leo Oppenheim, *Ancient Mesopotamia: Portrait of a Dead Civilization* (Chicago: University of Chicago Press, 1968, 1977). For more recent perspectives on the origins of Mesopotamian civilization, see Gwendolyn Leick, *Mesopotamia: The Invention of the City*, (New York: Penguin Books, 2003), and Harriet Crawford, *Sumer and the Sumerians* (2nd ed., Cambridge: Cambridge University Press, 2004).

[9] The earliest epigraphical mention of a people known as "Israel" is found on a victory stela erected by the Pharaoh Merneptah, ca. 1207 BCE, although scholarly consensus is lacking.

[10] For the Assyrian empire see Eckart Frahm, *The Assyrians: The Rise and Fall of the World's First Empire*; for the neo-Babylonian empire, see H. W. F. Saggs, *Babylonians* (Oakland, CA: University of California Press, 2000).

their sovereign's braggadocious exploits on victory stelae and palace walls. These accounts are certainly more propagandistic than biographical, but read critically, reliable historical information can be gleaned. Among these is a boastful account of the Assyrian King Sennacherib's campaign throughout the Levant in the late eighth century BCE, which also finds mention in the Bible. Imperial propaganda or not, this snapshot of kingship in the ancient world reveals the lofty arrogant mentality of royal power and offers an appropriate segue to the prophetic perspective on kingship in the next section:

> Sennacherib, the great king, the mighty king, king of the universe, king of Assyria, king of the four quarters of the earth; the wise ruler [lit. shepherd], favorite of the great gods, guardian of the right, lover of justice; who lends support and comes to the aid of the needy, who turns his thoughts to pious deeds; perfect hero, mighty man; first among all princes, the powerful one who consumes those who refuse to submit, who strikes the wicked with the thunderbolt; the god Assur, the great mountain, has entrusted to me an unrivaled kingship above all those who dwell in palaces and has made powerful my weapons; from the upper sea of the setting sun to the lower sea of the rising sun, he has placed all humankind [lit. "the black-headed people"] in submission at my feet.[11]

Monarchy in the Bible

The foundational narratives of the biblical Israelites depict foreign kings as formidable enemies to be overcome by Israel's warrior god, Yahweh, demonstrating his role in shaping world

---

[11] Adapted from Nels M. Bailkey and Richard Lim, *Readings in Ancient History*. 7th ed. (Boston: Cengage Learning, 2011 Boston, 2002), 59-60. The annals of Sennacherib's campaign throughout the Levant is recorded on three baked clay hexagonal stelae (and fragments of others). The most complete version, known as Taylor's Prism, was discovered in Nineveh (southern Iraq) in 1830 and is currently on display in the British Museum. Of particular interest are the lines describing Sennacherib's third campaign, which recounts the siege of Jerusalem in 701 BCE (cf. 2 Kgs 18:13-19:37 // Isa 36-37).

events through the control of its kings.[12] God delivers into
Abraham's hand the four Mesopotamian kings who attack the
Cities of the Plain and kidnap his nephew Lot (Gen 14:20); he
grants Moses victory over Pharaoh, the Amorite king Sihon,
and king Og of Bashan (Num 21:21-35); and he marches ahead
of Joshua in a lightning-quick conquest of thirty-one Canaanite
kings and their city-states (Jos 12:7-24). But upon their arrival
in Canaan, the tide begins to turn when the Israelites begin
forgetting [*shakach*] the Lord God who brought them up out of
the land of Egypt" (Deut. 4:9, 23; 6:12; 8:11, 14, 19; cf. 2 Kgs
17:38), setting in motion a tumultuous chain of events that leads
eventually to expulsion from the land God had granted them
tenancy upon.[13]

The ensuing period of conquest and settlement in Canaan
marks a transition in the role and function of foreign kings.
Kings of other nations, which previously had served as obstacles
to be mowed down before the arm of the Lord as a
demonstration of divine might, soon become formidable
instruments of chastisement for Israel's disobedience and lack of
trust in Yahweh. Joshua's failed assault against the city of Ai
(Joshua 7) shows how foreign kings who once fell before the
divine warrior of Israel would now be brought against God's
rebellious servants. Assyrian kings Tiglath-Pileser III ("Pul" in
2 Kgs 15:19) and Shalmaneser V are led westward to attack
Israel, destroy Samaria, and drive the recalcitrant Israelites into
exile (2 Kgs 18:11-12). Moreover, God brings the Babylonian
king Nebuchadnezzar against Jerusalem for the sins of King
Manasseh (2 Kgs 24:1-7). By contrast, but still making the point
that even the mightiest of earthly kings are but pawns, Cyrus
the Great, king of the Medes and Persians who the book of

---

[12] Listen to Fr. Paul Tarazi's explanation of the distinction between Yahweh and
Elohim on the Ephesus Network podcast series, *Tarazi Tuesdays*, Ep. 113
(April 14, 2020).
[13] See Tarazi's *Land and Covenant* (OCABS Press, 2009) for the biblical perspective on
the relationship between human beings and the earth, with implications for the
Israeli-Palestinian struggle today.

Isaiah hails as God's Anointed (*mashiach*, Isa 45:1-7), is summoned to Babylon to liberate the exiles, permitting them to return to Jerusalem where they soon demonstrate they have learned nothing from their previous experience.

The book of Judges, which is a second conquest narrative, contains stories that anticipate the establishment of the Israelite monarchy. Whatever sources the editors of the book of Judges may have had at their disposal, the text as we have it is largely anti-monarchical. Illustrative of this is the story of the mighty warrior Gideon, who after delivering his people from foreign invaders is invited by the Israelites to become king and establish his dynasty. However, he surprisingly acknowledges the sovereignty of the Lord by declining the opportunity:

> Then the Israelites said to Gideon, "Rule over us, you and your son and your grandson also, for you have delivered us out of the hand of Midian." Gideon said to them, "I will not rule over you, and my son will not rule over you; the Lord will rule over you." (Judg 8:22-23)

Gideon's affirmation of the Lord's sovereignty is rooted in remembrance of the Hebrews' deliverance from bondage in Egypt and their entrance into a covenant relationship with a new suzerain (cf. Exod 15:18; 19:3-6). His rejection of an opportunity to enjoy the wealth and power of a king seems uncanny and foreshadows the Lord's words to Samuel at the institution of the monarchy: "… for they have not rejected you but have rejected me as king over them" (1 Sam 8:7b). But the real lesson demonstrated by Gideon is the human failing he would have had as king when he transforms all the gold he takes as spoil into an ornate priestly vestment (*ephod*) that leads Israel into idolatry, for according to the prophetic perspective the object becomes a "snare" (*moqesh*) to Gideon and his house (Judg 8:27).

The anti-monarchical attitude continues with Abimelech, a son Gideon sires with a concubine, who upon his father's death allows Israel to continue its rampant idolatry. Abimelech, which ironically means "my father is king,"[14] rashly proclaims himself king of Israel (8:31) and proceeds to slaughter all his stepbrothers but one, "seventy men upon one stone" (Judg 9:5). Shortly afterward, the surviving son, Jotham, proclaims a lyrical parable from atop Mt. Gerazim, which Martin Buber deemed the strongest anti-monarchical poem ever written:[15]

> The trees went out at a time
> to anoint a king over themselves.
> And they said to the olive tree,
> "Come, reign over us."
> But the olive tree said to them,
> "Shall I leave my fatness
> by which God and men are honored
> to go and rule over the trees?"
> Then the trees said to the fig tree,
> "Come, reign over us."
> But the fig tree answered them,
> "Shall I leave my sweetness
> and my good fruit
> to go and rule over the trees?"
> Then the trees said to the vine,
> "Come, reign over us."
> But the vine said to them,
> "Shall I stop producing my wine,
> which cheers gods and men and
> and go to rule over the trees?"
> So all the trees said to the bramble,
> "Come, reign over us."
> And the bramble said to the trees,
> "If in truth you are anointing me king over you,
> then come and take refuge in my shade,
> but if not, let fire come out of the bramble
> and devour the cedars of Lebanon." (Judg 9:8-15)

---

[14] Not to be confused with Abimelech, king of Gerar (Gen 26:1-22; 26-31); or the son of David's high priest Abiathar (1 Chr 18:16), called Ahimelech in 2 Sam 8:17. Also, the name is also ascribed to every Philistine king from Abraham to David.

[15] Martin Buber, *Kingdom of God* (New York: Harper & Row, 1973), 75.

Jotham's ridicule of his murderous half-brother turns out to be oracular, for the Lord sends an evil spirit that divides Abimelech from his supporters. Soon a series of bloody battles ensues, in which Abimelech is mortally wounded by a skull-crushing stone dropped from a tower by a woman of Thebez. Suffering from a massive headache, but mostly fearful of the shame associated with being killed by a woman, Abimelech orders his armor bearer to administer the coup de grâce (vv. 53-54).

Other stories in the book of Judges seem to be more ambiguous in their attitude toward kingship. Scandalous and unsavory accounts like the horrific murder of the Levite's concubine (chs. 17-18) and the slaughter of the Benjaminites (chs. 19-21), which appear as appendices to the book, are linked by the leitmotif "In those days Israel had no king," framed by the observation that "every man did what was right in his own eyes" (17:6; 21:25). This leads many readers to suggest some imaginary time when the idea of having a monarchy was thought to be an antidote to widespread violence and idolatry; however, it is more likely the stories reflect a Judahite gibe against the failures of the charismatic and priestly leadership of the northern tribes to maintain law and order.[16] In any case, the statement about every man doing what was "right in his own eyes" overlooks the irony that such self-justified behavior is a distinctively royal prerogative that leads both nations along the path to eventual destruction and exile. It is also the case that the naïve notion a centralized ruler would solve Israel's problems anticipates the origin story of the monarchy in Samuel 8.

The transition from the Judges to the beginning of the Israelite monarchy recounted in Samuel 8 is ironic to the point of absurdity and clearly ahistorical. It begins with Samuel, the last of the judges, endeavoring to appoint his sons as successors to what was expected to be a charismatic, non-hereditary office:

---

[16] See Marvin Sweeny, "Davidic Polemics in the Book of Judges," *VT* 47 (1997): 517-529.

When Samuel became old, he appointed his sons as judges over Israel. The name of his firstborn son was Joel, and the name of his second, Abijah; they were judges in Beer-sheba. However, his sons did not follow in his ways but turned aside after gain, taking bribes and perverting justice. Then all the elders of Israel gathered together and came to Samuel at Ramah and said to him, "You are old, and your sons do not follow in your ways, so appoint for us a king to judge us like all the nations (1 Sam 8:1-5).

Careful readers will notice the two-pronged irony of the situation. First, why would the elders oppose Samuel's efforts to turn the traditionally charismatic leadership of the judges into a hereditary institution by requesting a form of government that is inherently dynastic? Their demand for a king simply makes no sense, for whatever corruption the sons could contrive as judges would be far easier to mitigate than acts of greed and injustice perpetrated by a greater centralized authority. The intractable despotism of kingship is illustrated in the story of Ahab and the disadvantaged Nabob (1 Kings 21), whose family estate is confiscated by the wicked king for no other reason than he desired to have it. Second, readers should note the absurdity of the biblical writer's explanation of the Israelite monarchy's origin, which does not come close to accounting how monarchies are formed. Consider the wide expanse of central Asia that includes modern-day Afghanistan, a region whose clans and tribal societies defy arbitrarily drawn boundaries and resist any centralization of authority. Independent tribal chieftains find little reason to coalesce around a common leader save in facing a common threat. These tribal alliances hold together for as long as a common threat remains but dissolve as soon as the trouble has passed. In sum, the biblical account of the monarchy's origin defies both history and common sense. The elders of Israel are intentionally presented as a naïve and misguided lot who double down on their request for a king, thereby rejecting God as king over them.

> Listen to the voice of the people in all that they say, for they have
> not rejected you, but they have rejected me as king over them.
> (1 Sam 8:7)

It should now be obvious that the Israelites' desire for a
human king to "be like other nations" is an act of rebellion
against the Lord's sovereignty. God's deliverance of the
Hebrews from slavery to the Egyptian Pharaoh does not mean
wholesale liberation, only a transference of servitude from one
king to another. The Lord condescends to the elders' rejection,
instructing Samuel to forewarn the elders concerning what is at
stake for their rebellion. Notice that the warning Samuel
delivers to the elders is dire and realistic, in contrast to the naïve
and unrealistic nature of their initial request for a king. The
English translation uses the repetitive cadence "he will take"
(*yiqqach*) and the pronominal suffix "his" to drive home the point
that the elders ought to reconsider their request:

> These will be the ways of the king who will reign over you: he will
> take your sons and appoint them to his chariots and to be his
> horsemen, and to run before his chariots; and he will appoint for
> himself commanders of thousands and commanders of fifties, and
> some to plow his ground and to reap his harvest, and to make his
> implements of war and the equipment of his chariots. He will take
> your daughters to be perfumers and cooks and bakers. He will
> take the best of your fields and vineyards and olive orchards and
> give them to his courtiers. He will take one-tenth of your grain
> and of your vineyards and give it to his officers and his courtiers.
> He will take your male and female slaves, and the best of your
> cattle and donkeys, and put them to his work. He will take one-
> tenth of your flocks, and you shall be his slaves. And in that day,
> you will cry out because of your king, whom you have chosen for
> yourselves; but the Lord will not answer you in that day.
> (vv. 10-18)

Still, the elders double down on their demand for a human king,
adding "that he may rule us and go out before us and fight our
battles." Here the irony intensifies, for at the time of year when
kings of other nations are leading their armies into battle, David

remains in Jerusalem (2 Sam 11:1). From there he proceeds to break eleven of the ten commandments in forty-eight hours' time, the most serious one being the first one—setting himself up uniquely as a god before God.

Samuel's realpolitik assessment of maintaining a centralized authority not only contrasts sharply with the naivete of the elders' request, but counters the Word of God regarding expectations for Israel's king:

> When you come into the land that the Lord your God is giving you to reside and settle in it, you say, "I will set a king over me, like all the nations that are around me." You may indeed set over you a king, one whom the Lord your God will choose. You may set one of your own kin as king over you, but you are not permitted to put a foreigner over you, one who is not of your own community. The king you appoint must not acquire an abundance of horses for himself, nor cause the people to return to Egypt for the purpose of acquiring more horses, since the Lord has said to you, "You must never return that way again." Neither shall he acquire many wives for himself or else his heart will turn away. Also, silver and gold he must not acquire in great quantity for himself. And it shall be that when he sits upon the throne of his kingdom, he shall write for himself a copy of this law on a scroll in the presence of the priests, the Levites. And it shall remain with him, and he shall read it all the days of his life that he may learn to fear the Lord his God, diligently observing all the words of this law and these statutes to do them, that his heart not be exalted above his fellows and that he not turn aside from the commandment, neither to the right nor to the left, that he may reign long in his kingdom, he and his children, in the midst of Israel. (Deut. 17:14-20)

While prophetic literature purports to be about the kingdoms of Israel and Judah, it should now be clear that something else is going on. The biblical story presents a rich pageant of failed kings that lead their nations down the path toward eventual destruction. Such texts can hardly be called royal annals, given that significant achievements of powerful kings like Omri, Ahab, and Jehu, which are witnessed in the archaeological and historical records, are significantly downplayed, or completely ignored. The writer suggests that should readers desire more information, they can consult various royal annals available at the time, sources that have not survived the merciless march of history.

The manipulation of the story of biblical Israel's past is evident in the post-destruction revision of the Deuteronomistic history (Dtr²), which significantly altered the portraits of Israel's and Judah's kings. The original version, which was almost certainly written during Josiah's reign (640–609 BCE), is triumphalist, nationalistic, and predictably admiring of its kings. As royal propaganda, it would not have stood the test of time, probably not much longer than the death of its crowning hero, King Josiah. Coming to grips with the unexpected death of the king who reformed and centralized Yahwistic religion and promulgated the Law of Moses throughout the land must have been difficult. As monumental a task that must have been,

> Still, the Lord did not turn away from the heat of his fierce anger, which burned against Judah because of all that Manasseh had done to arouse his anger. So the Lord said, "I will remove Judah also from my presence as I removed Israel, and I will reject Jerusalem, the city I chose, and this temple, about which I said, 'My Name shall be there.'" (2 Kgs 23:26-27)

Jerusalem's conquest at the hands of the Babylonians and their Edomite mercenaries just twelve years later, and the temple's destruction roughly twelve years after that, required serious wrangling with the question of what had gone so terribly wrong that Yahweh would permit his city and house to be destroyed. Was this not the same God who had delivered Jerusalem from the Assyrians roughly a century earlier? What had changed? Instead of writing history as a chain of natural causation, they composed an ultimate history for Jerusalem's demise. A regular historian would observe that the Babylonians destroyed Jerusalem, but ultimate history ascribes supernatural causation to the event; that is, Yahweh destroyed Jerusalem using the Babylonians as his rod of chastisement.

As a way of making sense of things, the scribes exposed the nation to the prophets' rigorous assessment of the nation charging it with the responsibility for what had gone so terribly wrong. Taking up the pen, the story of Israel's past was revised, especially as regards its kings. Legendary materials portraying Saul as a tall and handsome warrior, David as a valiant shepherd boy who could slay a lion with his bare hands, and Solomon as an incredibly wealthy paragon of wisdom are still apparent in the text. However, after the destruction, this triumphalist royal saga was transformed into a self-critical retrospective (Dtr[2]) that enables the work to survive. In fulfilment of its unique function in accounting for what went wrong, it presents the monarchy for what it was—a dismal repository of misplaced trust in kings who marched their nations toward their eventual demise. Building on the earlier, triumphalist royal saga, the prophetically influenced story of Israel's inglorious past retains its earlier details to illustrate just how far kings can fall. Saul the Benjaminite, a tall and handsome warrior, spirals into paranoid schizophrenia and ends his life by suicide; David, the brave shepherd boy who kills a lion with his bare hands and slays a formidable Philistine, goes on to break pretty much all the commandments in forty-eight hours' time; and Solomon's incomparable wisdom all but completely dissipates in the face of royal polyamory, idolatry, and despotism. The result is a parade of literary characters whose imputed weaknesses and terminal failures make them appear more realistic (and more interesting) than their actual historical prototypes.

The David and Uriah the Hittite story (2 Samuel 11) provides one of the best examples of the prophetic critique of monarchy. It begins by calling to mind the reason Israel implored Samuel for a king in the first place, namely, to be "like other nations" and have a king to fight their battles (1 Sam 8:20). However,

At the return of the year [*l'teshubah ha-shanah*; that is, Spring, the agricultural new year], the time when kings [of other nations] go out to battle, David sent Joab, his servants, and all Israel with him. They destroyed the Ammonites and besieged Rabbah, but David remained in Jerusalem.

The story relates that late in the afternoon David arises from his couch and ambles about on the roof of the palace. As he peers down over the wadi Kidron, he spies a woman bathing; finding her beautiful, he demands to know who she is. David learns that she is Bathsheba, the wife of a soldier who is away fighting in the Ammonite war, the king summons his messengers to bring her to the palace, whereupon he lies with her and impregnates her.[17] Like Judah, eponymous ancestor of his tribe (Gen 38:20-23), David is desperate to cover his tracks lest his deeds garner shame. He sends a message to his cousin Joab, commander of Israel's army, summoning Uriah to the palace. When the soldier arrives, David feigns interest in Uriah's take on the status of the war with the Ammonites. As a character Uriah has full agency, but the narrator is not forthcoming concerning what Uriah must be thinking. Is the warrior confused and oblivious to what is going on? Surely he must be harboring suspicion; however, the text does not say either way. It only relates that when Uriah is invited to go home to his wife and "wash his feet" (euphemistically speaking), he remains within the palatial precinct and sleeps in the servants' quarters in the chambers of the gate, perhaps sharing with them the food David had sent along with him. The following

---

[17] It is worth noting here that Bathsheba is what literary critics call a "flat character" in that she has no agency. Intentional gaps in the narrative prevent the reader from knowing whether she is a hapless victim of the king's power or may be planning the entire course of events to become part of the royal house. However, the scales later tip in favor of the latter when she explicitly negotiates the accession of her son Solomon to the throne (1 Kgs 1:15-40), whereupon her machinations not only secure the throne for her son but elevate her to the exalted status of queen mother (*gebirah*). Thus, the present story should not be referred to as the David and Bathsheba story as it is traditionally, but the David and Uriah the Hittite story, given both characters are equally dynamic and meant to be juxtaposed for contrast.

morning, when questioned why he declined the king's invitation to go home, Uriah reasons:

> The ark and Israel and Judah are dwelling in tents, and my commander Joab and Your Majesty's servants are encamped in the open field. Who am I, that I should go to my house to eat and drink and lie with my wife? As you live, and as your soul lives, I will not do such a thing. (v. 11)

The irony here is obvious. Uriah's loyalty to his fellow soldiers contrasts sharply with David's neglect. Even though Uriah bears a Yahwistic theophoric name (that is, a name that bears the name of Israel's national god, here likely meaning "Yahweh is my light"), he still carries a Hittite ethnic identity marker indicating non-Israelite ancestry. Uriah is married to an Israelite woman and is listed among David's thirty-seven elite warriors (*gibborim*; 2 Sam 23:29); however, his loyalty and worth as a valiant warrior seems to be of little importance to the king in light of his urgent need to avert the potential damage to his reputation. Ruthless kings often do whatever they please, openly and with no concern about what others think, but David is expressly concerned with covering up his misdeeds, demonstrating an awareness that he is expected to uphold the law of God and nation.

Having failed in the first attempt to get Uriah to go home, he invites the soldier to a feast and gets him drunk, thinking this time he might be persuaded to go home and sleep with his wife; however, Uriah maintains his loyalty and remains with the palace servants in the chambers of the gate (v. 13). It may be hard for some to imagine why Uriah would not take advantage of the opportunity extended to him. After all, what difference would it make to his fellow soldiers? But he himself would know. His character is adorned with greater honor than the king. When all has failed, David sends Uriah back with his own death sentence—a note to Joab ordering him to place the loyal soldier at the forefront of the fighting that he may be killed. With blind obedience, Joab does so, even at the cost of additional casualties.

Joab sends a battle report back to the king, apparently unsure what sort of reaction the news would evoke. Suspecting that the note he received might offer insurance against the king's anger, he tells the messenger to punctuate the report with news that Uriah the Hittite is dead. The messenger fulfills his mission, and upon believing he has been relieved of his problem, David replies with nonchalance, "Tell Joab not to worry, for the sword devours one way and the other" (v. 25), in other words, "Well, you win some, you lose some."

The narrative symmetry of David's and Uriah's contrasting characters and actions, the crescendo of flux arising from that tension, and the obvious affront to justice (a departure from 2 Sam 8:15: "And David administered justice and equity to all his people") serve to demonstrate that this is not intended to be interpreted as history, but as a literary production intended to make the point that even the most celebrated of Israel's kings were not equipped to deliver a disobedient people from divine judgment. David manages to break most, if not all the commandments, and while he acknowledges the consequences in the death of his child with Bathsheba, there is no indication of repentance, leaving the writer of Psalm 51 to fill that scandalous omission sometime later. However, of all the commandments David manages to break, it is the first of the ten that is most dangerous. By acting uniquely, David sets himself up as a god in defiance of the law, thereby breaking the commandment "You shall have no other gods before me" (Exod 20:3). Whenever persons in positions of responsibility set themselves above the law of God, they break the first commandment, and whenever the first commandment is broken, the rest will tumble like dominoes.

Solomon, David's surviving son and heir, provides another example of the utter failure of Israel's kings to deliver Judah from destruction and exile. The earlier material, which would have had no reason to survive were it not for the post-destruction revision that pulled together the core of the Bible as

Bible (see Introduction), lauds the king as wealthy and powerful, a paragon of wisdom, and the builder of Jerusalem's temple. But by the end of his life, Solomon becomes a grave idolator because of all his marriage alliances to foreign women, and a despotic exploiter of labor calling to mind the Pharaoh of the Exodus in the use of forced labor (*mas*). Also telling is the fact that Solomon spends nearly twice the amount of time building his own much larger royal palace than it took to build as the Temple (1 Kgs 7:1-9).

One obvious revision to the story of Solomon includes the addition of a second dream following construction of the temple. The two dreams are quite different and raise the question of why a second dream—one that detracts from the temple's glory—was needed (1 Kgs 3:5-14; 9:1-9). In the first dream, Yahweh appears to Solomon and asks him what he should like to receive from the Lord. With a humility not at all characteristic of royalty, the king asks solely for the gift of wisdom sufficient to rule his people (3:5-9). Pleased with Solomon's request, Yahweh grants the king great wisdom and promises so much more, namely, all the things he might otherwise have asked for (vv. 10-14):

> Because you have asked this and have not asked for yourself long life, or riches, or for the life of your enemies, but have asked for yourself understanding to discern justice, I now do according to your word. Indeed, I give you a wise and discerning mind so that no one like you has been before you and no one like you shall arise after you. I also give you what you have not asked, both riches and honor all your days such that no other king shall compare with you. If you walk in my ways, keeping my statutes and my commandments as your father David walked, then I will lengthen your days. (1 Kgs 3:11-14)

But here the question arises: Which David are we talking about? Is it the handsome young shepherd boy who slays lions and Philistines by his own hand? Or the covetous adulterer and murderer who sets himself high above the law as a god? The positive layer that introduces Israel's earliest monarchs is understandably predictable, purely ideological, and the sort of thing one would expect to read inscribed on a tablet dug up from any Near Eastern archaeological site. Yet somehow, Solomon's wisdom is heralded as the greatest among all the rulers of the earth, enshrined in the books of Proverbs, Ecclesiastes, the Song of Solomon, and the Wisdom of Solomon, as well as later texts like the *Psalms of Solomon* and the *Odes of Solomon*.

> And God gave Solomon exceeding wisdom and understanding, as well as greatness of heart, to the extent of sand upon the seashore. And Solomon's wisdom exceeded the wisdom of all the children of the East and all the wisdom of Egypt. For he was wiser than all men [. . .] and his fame was known to all nations round about. And he spoke 3,000 proverbs and composed 1,005 songs. He spoke about trees—from the cedar that is in Lebanon to the hyssop that sprouts from the wall; he spoke also of beasts and birds, creeping things and fish. And people came from all around to hear the wisdom of Solomon, from all kings of the earth who had heard of his wisdom. (1 Kgs 5:9-14)

It is almost certain that this royal legendary paean would have disappeared into the dustbin of history had it not become linked to a different sort of project linking it to the remembrance of a nation and the reason why its history had come to a full stop. This is why the foundation narrative of Solomon's temple comes to be framed by a second dream, a prophecy *ex eventu* that provides explanation for what had gone so terribly wrong that Solomon's grand and glorious temple would come to be destroyed. The second dream is so specific in its description of what would happen should the nation go astray that it can only be a *fait accompli* for the biblical writer:

> If you turn aside from following me, you or your children, and do not keep my commandments and my statutes that I have set before you, but go and serve other gods and worship them, then I will cut off Israel from the land that I have given them; and the house that I have consecrated for my name I will cast out of my sight; and Israel will become a proverb and a taunt among all

peoples. And this exalted house will become a heap of ruins;
everyone passing by it will be astonished, and will hiss, saying,
"Why has the Lord done such a thing to this land and to this
house?" Then they will say, "Because they have forsaken the
Lord their God, who brought their ancestors out of the land of
Egypt, and embraced other gods, worshipping them and serving
them; therefore, the Lord has brought this disaster upon them."
(1 Kgs 9:6-9)

Other clues in the story of Solomon indicate that it is not so
much a royal annal as an ironic parable. Oddly, of all the
generous affirmations heaped upon Solomon for representing
the wisest of all rulers only one clear example is provided,
namely the well-known story of the two prostitutes claiming to
be mothers of a single baby (1 Kgs 3:16-28). One cannot know
whether all of Solomon's wise acts "from first to last," were
really recorded in "the history of the prophet Nathan, the
prophecy of Ahijah the Shilonite, or in the Visions of the seer
Iddo" as the Chronicler attests (2 Chr 9:29) but by relating only
one example, the royal tradition is seriously challenged in light
of such hyperbolic praise.

Yet another popular aspect of Solomon's character is his
exorbitant wealth, which like his wisdom exceeds that of "all the
kings of the earth" (1 Kgs 10:23; 2 Chr 9:22) and equally
exaggerated beyond absurdity, especially by the Chronicler:

Now the weight of gold that came to Solomon in one year was
666 talents [approximately 24 tons] in addition to the taxes paid
by traders and merchants. And the kings of Arabia and the
governors of the Israelite districts also brought him silver and
gold. And Solomon made 200 large shields of beaten gold, each
one covered with 600 shekels [roughly fifteen pounds] of beaten
gold, and 300 smaller shields, each covered with about 300
shekels of beaten gold. He had them all placed in the house of the
forest of Lebanon. Moreover, the king made a great throne of
ivory and overlaid it with pure gold. Six steps led up to the throne,
and there was a footstool of gold also attached to it. There were
arms on each side of the throne, with two lions standing at each
side. And twelve lions stood on one side and the other upon the

six steps. No throne like this had ever been made in any other kingdom. (2 Chr 19:13-19)

In addition to Solomon's unparalleled wisdom and wealth, he is described as an emperor over a vast empire comprising an area of approximately 75,000 square miles:

Solomon was sovereign over all the kingdoms from the Euphrates to the land of the Philistines, even to the border of Egypt; they brought tribute and served Solomon all the days of his life. (1 Kgs 4:24-26; 10:26)

Solomon's purported harem of 1,000 women also speaks to the power, might, and glory accorded to an epic ruler; however, this bit of triumphalist royal propaganda has been edited to cast great shame upon the king. One could argue that some of Solomon's consorts were the daughters of foreign kings married for purposes of ensuring stable political and economic alliances among nations—a certain kind of savvy, perhaps—but how can one reconcile Solomon's true God-given wisdom with his public display of rampant idolatry? Setting up high places (*bamoth*) in Jerusalem for the worship of gods like Chemosh, supreme god of the Moabites, and Molech, god of the Ammonites (2 Kgs 11:7) exposes Solomon's accommodation of these detestable abominations (*shiqqutz*), offering a reasonable explanation for why God divides the kingdom after his death:

Wherefore the Lord said to Solomon, "For as much as this has been in your mind, and you have not kept my covenant and the statutes I have commanded you I will surely tear the kingdom from you and will give it to your servant. (v.11)

The epic portrayal of a grand and glorious Israelite empire is seriously challenged by the historical and archaeological record. The oft-repeated conservative refrain "absence of evidence is not evidence of absence" is weak given the preponderous evidence of absence surrounding a tenth-century BCE empire as described above. Like leftovers in the refrigerator, the excuse has pretty much surpassed its expiration date. It can be stated with confidence that if a Solomonic kingdom existed historically (to be sure, there is no reason to completely dismiss it), it could not have extended much beyond the walls of Canaanite Jerusalem. At any rate, there is not a hint of anything like it mentioned in extra-biblical sources and nothing definitively connecting it to any surrounding settlements as a centralized capital in the tenth-century BCE. Even the dating of gates at Hazor, Megiddo, and Gezer, attributed to Solomon in 1 Kgs 9:15 and long accepted as Solomonic for no real reason other than the Bible claims it, has been in serious dispute over many decades now.

It is almost certainly the case that the Deuteronomistic account of Israel's past, a Judahite production, took advantage of having the last word, magnifying its own Davidic dynasty over the historically original and more dominant northern kingdom, which had come to end in 722 BCE. After all, has anyone not wondered why a putative break-away, non-Davidic kingdom of Israel (1 Kings 12) should retain the name "Israel," leaving the Davidic-Solomonic dynasty to resort to the tribal name "Judah."? Moreover, as Israeli archaeologist Norma Franklin has noted, mason's marks on ashlars traditionally identified with Solomonic architecture tie these monuments to the northern kingdom of Omri and Ahab.[18] It would be safe to say the absence of evidence for Solomon's vast biblical empire argues strongly in favor of historical absence.

Having said this, it is the case that a fragmentary Aramaic inscription discovered out of context at Tel Dan in 1994 provides evidence that a "house of David" once existed, that is, a late ninth-century BCE dynasty that traced its lineage back to someone called "David," a name that derives from the Hebrew "beloved." However, one must accept the inscription for what it is, simply a shard with the name of a kingdom otherwise unknown in the material record. It should not be accepted as evidence for the full-blown empire described by later Judahite authors following the demise of the norther kingdom. The

---

[18] Norma Franklin, "Lost Tombs of the Israelite Kings," *BAR* 33/34 (2007): 26-35.

inscription simply witnesses to the victory of an Aramean king, likely Hazael, over two enemies from the south, a "king of Israel" and a king of the "house of David" (*beit dwd*). It says nothing about the extent of these polities, let alone anything about David as a person.[19]

Unlike the house of David and Solomon, the ninth-century BCE house of Omri (*bit hu-um-ri-a*) is well attested in various cuneiform sources outside the Bible. The Omride dynasty appears to have been something of a powerhouse in Syria-Palestine, given that its name remained synonymous with the northern kingdom of Israel even after its end. The house of Omri is mentioned in the so-called Moabite inscription, which was copied from a ninth-century BCE stela discovered in Dhiban, Jordan (biblical Dibon) in 1868, currently on display in the Louvre. It recounts king Mesha's success in entreating the deity Chemosh to help end the house of Omri's occupation of his land, which occurred as punishment for the Moabites' lapse of devotion for their national god. The inscription relates Mesha's victory against the "son of Omri," most likely Ahab, and other foreign enemies. The Moabite king is mentioned in the Bible as a breeder of sheep (*noqem*)[20] who pays the Omrides seasonal tributes of "one hundred thousand lambs, along with the wool of one hundred thousand rams," and continues to pay tribute until Ahab's death, at which time he rebels

---

[19] Avraham Biran and Joseph Naveh, "An Aramaic Stele Fragment from Tel Dan," *IEJ* 43 (1993): 81–98; also, "The Tel Dan Inscription: A New Fragment," *IEJ* 45 (1995): 1-18. The interpretation of the fragment is debated among scholars who suggest a word divider is lacking, thus allowing for other possible meanings. See Philip R. Davies, "'House of David' Built on Sand: The Sins of the Biblical Maximizers," *BAR* 20 no. 4 (1994), with a scathing rejoinder by Anson Rainey, "The 'House of David' and the House of the Deconstructionists," *BAR* 20.6 (1994): 47.Similarly, line 31 of the Mesha inscription of the Moabite stone may also refer to a *beit dwd*, but crucial letters are missing, and scholars are far from any sort of agreement over what they represent.

[20] Mesha is described as a *noqed*, a rare Hebrew word that refers to a dealer in sheep. Apart from Mesha, the only other time it appears is in the superscription of the book of Amos, who is said to have been among the *noqedim* of Tekoa (although in 7:14 he is called *boker*, from *bakar*, for cattle or oxen).

(2 Kgs. 3:4-5). Another significant extrabiblical witness to the House of Omri is found on the so-called Black Obelisk discovered in Nimrud in the mid-nineteenth century. The stela bears a relief of a king identified as Jehu (*Yehu*), son of Omri (*Humri*) kneeling in obeisance before Shalmaneser III. The biblical account identifies Jehu as having murdered Ahab and all his family (2 Kgs 10:17), thus bringing an end to the House of Omri, but the Assyrians were apparently oblivious to such details.

There are yet other extrabiblical references to the House of Omri that indicate the strength of the dynasty. On display in the British Museum are two Assyrian stele (monoliths), discovered in 1861 near Kurkh (Üçtepe), Türkiye, that recount the military exploits of Assyrian kings Ashurnasirpal II and his son, Shalmaneser III. One of the stelae recounts Shalmaneser III's defeat by a twelve-nation coalition at the battle of Qarqar (although only eleven kingdoms appear to be listed), fought along the banks of the Orontes River in 853 BCE. According to the inscription, the coalition was co-led by the Aramean king Hadad-ezer and a king named *A-ha-ab-bu Sir-ila-a-a*, who most scholars identify as Ahab of Israel.[21] It attributes to Ahab 2,000 chariots of iron—more than half of all the other nations' iron chariots combined—as well as 10,000 infantrymen. This significant military contribution to the Syrian coalition apparently won the day, for its Pyrrhic victory managed to stall the Assyrian advance for the next few battle seasons.

The fact that the Assyrians would acknowledge such a defeat is noteworthy. The glorification of kings, their wealth, and their exploits is a common characteristic of literature in the ancient Near East; however, the Bible as Bible, on its way toward becoming scripture, has no interest in promoting royal ideology.

---

[21] Scholars who cast doubt on this interpretation point to the fact that other known Assyrian (and Babylonian) inscriptions (e.g., the Moabite stela) identify Israel as the House of Omri (*bit hu-um-ri-a*). It does not appear to be a very strong argument, given the strength of the transliteration, geographical context, and relatively small sample.

There, Omri's dynasty, which is well attested in extrabiblical sources, is compressed into a handful of lines that all but ignore its monumental architecture and international renown:

> Omri bought the hill of Samaria from Shemer for two talents [*behikkerîm*] of silver. He built a city on it and called it Samaria [*shomeron*] after the name of Shemer, owner of the hill. But Omri did what was evil in the Lord's sight, more than any of the kings before him, for he walked in the ways of Jeroboam son of Nebat in the sin by which he made Israel to sin, provoking the anger of the Lord God of Israel with their idols. The rest of the acts that Omri did, and the might [*geburah*] that he showed, are they not recorded in the book, words of the chronicles [lit. the days, *hayamim*] of the kings of Israel? (1 Kgs 16:24-27)

Clearly the wealth and power of the House of Omri was of no concern to the biblical writer. He writes that readers interested in knowing more about Omri can look it up in the royal archives (1 Kgs 16:27). Much more is written in the Bible concerning Omri's son, Ahab, but the scribe is no less dismissive of his exploits because it also subverts the prophetic agenda. In contrast to the robust military resources ascribed to him on the Moabite inscription and the Shalmaneser III stela, biblical Ahab is summarily written off as a corrupt, idolatrous, unjust, and murderous king:

> And Ahab, son of Omri, did evil in the eyes of the Lord more than all the other [kings] before him. And it came to pass, as though it had been a trivial thing for him to walk in the ways of Jeroboam son of Nebat, that he took Jezebel, daughter of king Ethbaal of the Sidonians, for his wife, and went and worshiped and served Baal. And he set up an altar for Baal in the temple of Baal, which he had built in Samaria. Ahab set up a wooden image [*asherah*] and did more to provoke the Lord to anger than all the kings of Israel who were before him (1 Kgs 16:30-33).

On the basis of archaeological evidence, it is safe to say that the Omride dynasty left a profound imprint in Levantine domestic and international affairs—something one would never know by reading the Bible alone.

Prophetic literature is equally critical of foreign kings. Self-assumed grandeur on the part of ancient Near Eastern kings is evidenced by the adoption of epithets like "King of All" or "King of the Universe," which appear in cuneiform records over several centuries—from Akkadian kings Sargon and Naram-Sin in the third millennium BCE to neo-Assyrian and neo-Babylonian destroyers of Samaria and Judah in the first millennium BCE. As the text of Sennacherib's victory stela above shows, royal status and power comes from the gods, but the God of scripture belittles the great kings of the earth:

> How you are fallen from the skies,
> O Morning Star, son of the dawn!
> How you are cut down to the ground,
> you who took nations captive!
> And you said in your heart,
> "I will ascend to the heavens;
> Above the stars of God
> will I raise my throne;
> I will sit upon the mount of assembly
> in the highest heights of the north;
> I will ascend high above the clouds
> and be like the Most High."
> But you shall be brought down to Sheol,
> to the lowest depths of the pit. (Isa 14:12-15)
> He that sits in the heavens laughs;
> the Lord holds them [the rulers of the earth] in derision (Ps 2:4)
>
> The Lord at your right hand will crush kings in the day of his wrath (Ps 110:5)

While titles like "King of All" is assumed by human kings in Mesopotamian royal archives, there are relatively few examples of "king" being applied to gods themselves. The Torah does not explicitly apply the title to God, although God is said to reign forever (Exod 15:18); however, prophetic literature and the Psalms advance the image liberally. King Hezekiah proclaims that the God of Israel is enthroned above the cherubim and rules over all the kingdoms of the earth (Isa 37:16). Isaiah proclaims:

Do you not know? Have you not heard? Has it not been told to you from the beginning? Have you not understood the foundations of the earth? It is he that sits above the circuit of the earth, the inhabitants of which are like grasshoppers, who stretches out the heavens as a curtain and spreads them out as a tent to dwell in, who makes the princes as nothing and makes the judges of the earth to naught. (Isa 40:21-23)

For God is King over all the earth. Sing praises in an artful song. God reigns over the nations; God sits upon his holy throne. (Ps 47:8-9)

For the Lord is a great God, and a great King above all gods. (Ps 95:3)

It should be clear that the biblical writers were clearly up to something other than providing a record of history as we understand it. The prophetic perspective asserts that kings are ultimately unable to offer any real protection in a dangerous or unpredictable world, which is what most people seem to want. In light of ultimate destruction, whether or not they come from the hand of God, kings simply cannot save:

I will destroy you, O Israel;
who can help you?
Where now is your king, that he may save you?
Where in all your cities are your rulers,
of whom you said,
"Give me a king and rulers"?
I gave you a king in my anger,
and I took him away in my wrath. (Hos. 13:9-11)

The Lord is king! Let the earth rejoice;
let the many coastlands be glad!
Clouds and thick darkness are all around him;
righteousness and justice are the foundation of his throne. (Ps 97:1-2)

The Lord has established His throne in the heavens; and His kingdom rules over all. (Ps 103:19)

The proclamation that the Lord is King is an example of how each element of the prophetic critique of human institutions covered in this book offers an ultimate divine counterpart. The rejection of Israel's kings asserts that the Lord himself is King, as reiterated throughout the Bible (e.g., Exod 15:18; Isa 37:16; 1 Chr 16:31, 29:12) and especially in the Psalms (e.g., Pss 9:7; 29:10; 45:6; 47:2; and elsewhere). At which point "king" becomes a metaphor for the God of Israel is debated in biblical scholarship. Was King and the language associated with kingship as applied to the Lord an early, pre-monarchic concept? Or was it a later development based on the model of Israel's monarchy or surrounding influences?[22] At any rate, it is the case that God is not explicitly referred to as *melek* in the Torah.

Unlike most royal annals of the ancient Near East, the prophetic critique of both Israelite and non-Israelite kings defies history in its own unique way even as it purports to recount it. Unfortunately, this leads readers to the naïve assumption that the biblical epic is a reliable account of history and geography and miss its primary message, namely that blind trust in human institutions—works of the hands—cannot deliver upon expectations. This applies to kingship as well, for despite all the celebrated (albeit violent) reforms carried out by Josiah, everything comes to an end when Josiah is felled by an Egyptian arrow. Hardly more than two decades later, the temple that Josiah renovated and gave exclusive legitimacy was brought to ruin, forcing the Deuteronomistic survivors to make sense of it all:

> Josiah put away the mediums, wizards, teraphim, idols, and all the abominations that were seen in the land of Judah and in Jerusalem, and he established the words of the law that were written in the book that the priest Hilkiah had found in the house of the Lord. Before him there was no king like him who turned to

---

[22] Marc Zvi Brettler, God as King: *Understanding an Israelite Metaphor* (Sheffield, UK: Sheffield Press, 1989); Shawn W. Flynn, *YHWH is King: The Development of Divine Kingship in Ancient Israel* (Leiden: Brill, 2013).

the Lord with all his heart, with all his soul, and with all his might, according to all the law of Moses, nor did any like him arise after him.

Still the Lord did not turn from the fierceness of his great wrath by which his anger was kindled against Judah because of all the provocations with which Manasseh had provoked him. The Lord said, "I will remove Judah also out of my sight, as I have removed Israel, and I will reject this city that I have chosen, Jerusalem, and the house of which I said, My name shall be there." (2 Kgs 23:24-26)

It is important to relinquish one's preconditioned expectations about the Bible in order to see more clearly what is going on. The point is clear that a bullet or an arrow can cut down a Josiah or a Lincoln, a Kennedy or a Rabin, and so on; so, placing one's trust in another human being to deliver upon things beyond their limits of life and power is foolishness at best. Equally naïve is the misplaced trust in so-called captains of industry and government to deliver the populace from the perils of future disasters like the widening global wealth gap and human-caused climate change.

Conclusion

It should be obvious by now that the biblical story of Israel's kings has far less to do with history, and everything to do with what it means to be in a position of authority. We have seen the accomplishments of biblical kings of Israel and Judah—some of which evidenced by history—are altogether ignored, downplayed, or significantly distorted so that whatever successes or failures kings of history may have actually had, human rulers in the biblical story are consigned to collective failure. Biblical writers could not erase certain remembrances out of national history, but they could interpret them as they saw fit—in this case showcasing leaders for their inability to deliver the nation from destruction and exile, let alone live upright responsible lives! To the prophetically influenced priestly scribes, the very idea of monarchy was anathema from the start for its rejection of God as King, who brought them up out of the land of Egypt (1 Sam 8:7-8). Its parade of kings marches on to oblivion: Samaria for the sins of Jeroboam; Jerusalem for the sins of Manasseh.

The political concept of autocracy poses no problem in itself—only the way unconstrained rule in the hands of a single individual tends to play out in the world. It tends to nourish certain identity cults with rallying cries of victimization and loss of status, while creating unjust and sometimes perilous situations for actual victims of marginalized society. To be sure, other forms of government can be similarly oppressive; for as human constructs all political systems, imbued with human imperfections, have their faults. Nevertheless, despots of the past are often remembered kindly by history, and the hope for a wise, just, and righteous king continues to inspire the human psyche so that people of all eras fall prey to hope for a savior. At the end of the day, Lord Acton's timeless, oft-repeated axiom remains relevant: "Power tends to corrupt, and absolute power corrupts absolutely," and, as the quote continues, "Great men are almost always bad men." But at the end of the day, the problem lies not with kings themselves, but with the foolish investment of trust placed in them by everyday people out of fear and insecurity and lack of faith in the divine King and Shepherd. Perhaps the well-known quote from Walt Kelly's *Pogo* comic strip is even more appropriate, "We have met the enemy and he is us." The Bible as scripture demands that its hearers behave responsibly within each our own personal realms—in family relationships, social organizations, political office, and so on—obliterating the ego to manifest the kingdom of God on earth through obedience to the heavenly King and mercy toward one's neighbor.

Chapter 3
The Trouble with Cities

Then Cain went away from the presence of the Lord [...] and he built a city and called the name of the city after the name of his son Enoch (Gen 4:16-17)

Judah has multiplied its fortified cities, but I will send a fire upon them that will devour all their strongholds (Hos 8:14)

Currently, more than half the world's inhabitants reside in or around cities, usually defined as places where people of different backgrounds reside in proximity to one another for the purpose of meeting particular needs or desires.[1] To be sure, the city has become the dominant socioeconomic influence on human life globally, significantly affecting rural populations of the world as well. In recent years, accelerated growth in the number and size of cities, especially in Africa and Asia, has raised serious challenges for the future of all humanity.[2] Of particular concern is the rising number of displaced persons affected by war, natural disasters, and climate change seeking refuge in cities around the world. As we lounge comfortably in our living rooms, the number of persons in the world being forcefully displaced from their homes due to conflict or natural disaster is surpassing 110 million, of which more than 35 million

---

[1] In other words, heterogeneity plus density equals urbanism, a formula that stems from the seminal work on urban population studies, Louis Wirth's "Urbanism as a Way of Life," AJS 44.1 (1938): 1-24. See also Harvard economist Edward Glaeser's *Triumph of the City* (Penguin, 2011).

[2] All population data is from "World Urbanization Prospects," UN Department of Economic and Social Affairs: https://population.un.org/wpp/. The most urgent concern is the human effect on climate change, which has led some scientists to mark the transition from the stable climate of the Holocene period to the geological hazards of the Anthropocene age, a term was coined in 2000 by biologist Eugene Stormer and chemist Paul Crutzen to refer to the present era, in which human activity exerts a measurable impact on established terrestrial climate norms and ecosystems. See Erle C. Ellis, *The Anthropocene: A Very Short Introduction* (Oxford: Oxford University Press, 2018); Julia Adeney Thomas, Mark Williams, and Jan Zalasiewicz, *The Anthropocene: A Multidisciplinary Approach* (Cambridge, UK: Polity, 2020).

are refugees seeking shelter in cities already straining to provide basic needs in housing, employment, sanitation, security, and transportation.[3]

It may be all too easy for people to ignore the plight of human beings struggling to survive in stiflingly crowded cities tens of thousands of miles away, but how can privileged society overlook the suffering of the poor and homeless in our own cities? The irony is that the larger and grander our cities become, the more their rising structures of glass and steel alienate us from the natural world, from one another, and thus ultimately from ourselves. While some urban planners seek to ameliorate the situation by incorporating common green spaces into their layouts, these zones are often lined with Starbucks kiosks, Apple stores, and Louis Vuitton outlets aimed at attracting today's millennial-generation urban professionals ("Muppies"). The lives of penthouse dwellers in gentrified high-rise districts from Manhattan to San Francisco remain at far remove from the plight of homeless veterans and runaway teens shivering in cardboard boxes in alleys and doorways below. If there is anything inherently amiss with the institution of the city, it is the broad chasm of socioeconomic disparity that divides citizens across micro-spatial confines and ghettos. Such is the insidiously dark side of the city, where mentally ill, hungry, exploited, and otherwise marginalized persons huddle invisibly in shadowed alleyways and beneath bridges—a pervasive and largely unaddressed urban miasma more toxic than pollution, high taxes, or crime. The plight of the poor and homeless is not a problem to be solved by building walls, as politicians sometimes suggest. But bold and serious thinking about what it means to live scripturally in an urbanized world—engaging prophetic principles of justice and righteousness (*mishpat ve-*

---

[3] United Nations High Commissioner for Refugees data available at https://www.unhcr.org/what-we-do/reports-and-publications/unhcr-data. International Rescue Committee website: https://www.rescue.org/topic/refugee-crisis

tzedakah) toward all—requires that the problems faced by poor and marginalized persons among us be taken up as our own.[4]

The problems for comfortable urban dwellers are less obtuse but may be insidious in other ways. Taking the benefits of urban life for granted, many just plug themselves into the matrix, mindlessly following routine paths through nameless crowds on the way to their office or boutique, giving little thought to the mechanics and infrastructure that keep things humming predictably around them. Their thoughts are immediate and reactive, rarely thoughtfully responsive, perhaps flashing back and forth between feelings of civic pride at passing the construction site of a new sports arena or convention center, or disdain at the thought of the greater tax hikes and traffic jams it will bring. What gets missed in all the bustle is that the unconscious sense of security and well-being is ultimately transient and illusory.

The aim of this admittedly bleak introduction is not to disparage urban life, or even the city itself, but to think about the city in the larger context of the human condition; for whatever one's attitude toward cities today, archaeological sites around the world bear silent witness to their inevitable demise. No earthly city is eternal. In fact, if archaeology and scripture agree on anything, it is the indisputable fact that even the most vibrant and defensible cities enjoy but fleeting existence upon the earth. Following a brief look at the historical and archaeological picture of ancient cities, we explore the biblical perspective to appreciate the stark contrast presented by the Prophets, who peer beyond the illusory nature of the city to expose the consequences of trusting in idols of concrete and steel.

---

[4] Glasser, Edward L, Matthew E. Kahn, and Jordan Rappaport, "Why do the Poor Live in Cities? The Role of Public Transportation." *JUE* 63.1 (2008): 1-24.

The City in the Ancient Near East

It is a commonplace that Mesopotamia's earliest settlements were established roughly 10,000 years ago, as migratory hunters and pastoralists discovered agricultural processes and techniques and began settling down for extended periods of time.[5] More permanent settlements consisted of circular homes constructed of stacked reeds and mudbrick, which gave way to ceramic technology that further anchored a domestic lifestyle to the location. Working cooperatively, settlers labored to dig canals that would channel water for domestic use, increased animal husbandry, and the cultivation of grain, vines, and fruit-bearing trees.

As discussed in the previous chapter, settled populations began to grow larger and denser, creating the need for more complex social organization under a strong leader. By the sixth millennium BCE, a handful of large city-states began to emerge in the Sumerian region of southern Mesopotamia, including Eridu, Ur, Nippur, Lagash, Kish, and—the oldest and largest of them all—Uruk, located about two hundred miles south of present-day Baghdad, which had an estimated population somewhere between 40,000 and 80,000 persons.[6] These polities engaged one another in trade and sometimes warred among themselves. Their citizens, not all of which lived within their walls, must have appreciated their magnificence and impregnability while celebrating their respective patron deities.

---

[5] A city is a densely populated human settlement organized to meet the basic needs of its constituent society, usually characterized by human-made structures serving residential, administrative, cultural, and religious purposes. In ancient Mesopotamia, the rise of full-blown urban civilization emerges with Ubaid culture more than seven millennia ago. See Robert A. Carter and Graham Phillip, eds., *Beyond the Ubaid: Transformation and Integration in the Late Prehistoric Societies of the Middle East*. SAOC 63. Chicago: Oriental Institute, 2010.

[6] For a comprehensive look at the history, art, and architecture of Uruk, including its association with the *Epic of Gilgamesh*, see Nicola Crüsemann, Maragarete Van Ess, Markus Hilgert, et al., eds. *Uruk: First City of the Ancient World* (New York: J. Paul Getty Museum, 2019). For the rise of urban civilization in Mesopotamia generally, see Gwendolyn Leick, *Mesopotamia: The Invention of the City*, (New York: Penguin Books, 2003).

However, to the bands of migratory hunters and pastoralists who happened upon them, these unnatural bastions of elitist power arising from the landscape no doubt evoked a sense of wonder and foreboding.

Other Sumerian inventions besides these complex monumental settlements were bequeathed to their Akkadian, Babylonian, and Assyrian successors, who developed them even further. These include practical inventions like the wheel, the plow, beer, the sexagesimal system,[7] and others. The invention of writing, which came into use sometime around 3400 BCE, made accounting possible. Scribes employed a system of cuneiform symbols consisting of hundreds of wedge-shaped characters inscribed by a reed stylus on tablets of wet clay. These tablets were then baked in an oven or left in the sun to harden and are preserved to the present day. Finally, the invention of the alphabet in the early second millennium BCE allowed for greater nuance and versatility in writing, resulting in the production of law codes and literature, the latter including hymns and epics of human origins, heroes, and floods.

Among the vast number of Sumerian and Akkadian cuneiform tablets recovered in the modern period one finds hymns of praise for their monumental cities, including Babylon, Ashur, Kish, and Nippur. In various ways these royal paeans associate the city with the gods, either as divine gifts or royal tribute in appreciation for their sustained power and protection.[8] These mythic etiologies continued throughout the Bronze Age and into the Iron Age, maintained and nourished through ritual celebrations such as the biannual Akitu festival of Babylon, a lavish public observance devoted to the supreme god

---

[7] Although modified somewhat over time, the sexagesimal (base-60) system is still used today for measurements of time and space (coordinates and angles). Its facility arises from the fact that the number 60 is divisible by factors of 1, 2, 3, 4, 5, 6, 10, 12, 15, 20, 30, and 60.

[8] Ömür Harmanşah, *Cities and the Shaping of Memory in the Ancient Near East* (Cambridge: Cambridge University Press, 2015).

Marduk.[9] The intersection of grandiose kingship, fortified cities, and elaborate temples infused with the power of divinity certainly must have evoked an experience of utmost awe.

Narrowing the focus to the Levant, we find many cities that still bear toponyms that have survived in some form over millennia. These include Ashkelon (*Ashqelon*), Damascus (*Dammeseq*), Gaza (*Azzah*), Hebron (*Hebron*), Jericho (*Yericho*), Jerusalem (*Urushalim*), Sidon (*Tzaidan*), Tyre (*Tyros*), and others. While the names remain, the cities themselves do not, as many have endured intermittent phases of habitation, but not necessarily in the exact same location. Humans are resilient and form attachments to their homes and villages through personal investments of sweat, blood, and tears for the departed loved ones they buried nearby. Because of this, persons who were displaced by natural disaster or war almost always return to their homes and rebuild, that is, if possible to do so. Oftentimes, migrations and forced displacements due to climate change or war affect the ethnic make-up of cities. Assyrian cuneiform sources from the eighth-century BCE attest to deportations of some 50,000 Israelites from conquered cities like Samaria, Shechem, Bethel, and Gezer. As a result, hundreds of clay tablets found throughout modern day Iraq bear Hebrew personal names. Conversely, the Assyrians forcibly moved hundreds of thousands of refugees into the Levant from other corners of their empire. The fact that these displaced persons spoke different languages, observed different customs, and worshipped different gods enabled the Assyrian emperors to rule by confusion over the kingdoms they conquered, a strategy that allowed them to expand and maintain a vast empire.[10] All of this serves to indicate that Levantine cities were quite diverse

---

[9] H. W. F. Saggs, *Babylonians* (Berkeley: University of California Press, 2000), 131-32, 167.

[10] At Tel Gezer, clay tablets in Babylonian cuneiform dating to the early sixth-century BCE bear twenty-one presumably local names, twelve of which are Babylonian, five are West Semitic, one is Egyptian, and only one is Judahite. Other Babylonian names appear on ostraca from Samaria and elsewhere throughout Palestine.

and far more dynamic than the stability of their names would seem to indicate or their dominant cultural narratives would dare admit.

Although the names of cities may endure over millennia, it is important to realize that each represents not one but many cities, each one built atop another in layers of occupation over time, sort of like the layers of a cake. These levels, archaeological strata, witness to various natural and human-made disasters over time—earthquakes, floods, migrations, invasions, conquests, and so on—or additional fortifications on the part of kings. The ancient Canaanite city of Hazor (Arabic Tell al-Qedah), known in the Bible as "the head of all those kingdoms" (Josh 11:10), comprises more than twenty-one strata spanning almost three millennia. Tel Megiddo, rising above the southern end of the Jezreel Valley roughly fifty miles southwest of Hazor, boasts up to twenty-six occupation levels. It witnesses to the Chalcolithic period (4500–3300 BCE), two systemic collapses during the Bronze Age, conquests by a succession of Canaanite, Egyptian, Philistine, and Assyrian kings, and final destruction by the Babylonian king Nebuchadnezzar in the early sixth century BCE.[11]

These and many other cities are mentioned in the Bible; however, it is not always possible to match their names to actual archaeological sites. The science of archaeology has been compromised by faithful Jews and Christians who rely too heavily on the Bible as a reliable source of history and geography. This abuse has been especially egregious in the exclusivist politics of modern Israel's nation-building, which conservative Christians tend to support. Here is not the place to deal with this problem, except to say that proper identification of biblical sites depends on fulfilling one of three criteria: The

---

[11] For an imaginative journey through a succession of cities at a single site from Neolithic to the Crusader period, see James A. Michener's *The Source* (New York: Random House, 1965). Although the fictional Tell Makor's latest occupation level dates to the turn of the thirteenth century, critical readers may detect the book's pro-Israeli apologetic.

first is the rare chance of finding an ostracon (an inscribed shard of pottery) attesting to the name of the city, such as the famous bilingual Greek and Aramaic inscription found at Tel Dan in 1976 that reads, "To the God who is in Dan." A second criterion depends on exact identification in extra-biblical sources, such as Josephus's placement of Bethsaida-Julias near the eastern shore of the Jordan River where it empties into the Sea of Galilee (*The Jewish War* 3.10.7). The third criterion, the most likely to be found, depends on the preservation in Arabic of the site's name, such as Khirbet Seilun for biblical Shiloh, or Tel el-Jazar for biblical Gezer.[12] Thus, identification of a biblical site made on the basis of the Bible alone is at best conjectural and methodologically flawed.[13]

Although the names of many known cities appear in the Bible, it is clear they cannot be relied upon for accurate historical or geographical information. One example is Jericho, the first city to be conquered by Joshua and the Israelites upon their entrance into Canaan. One of the oldest continuously inhabited cities in the world, Jericho (Arabic Tell es-Sultan) was excavated by British archaeologist John Garstang in the early 1930s. Heavily influenced by reliance upon the Bible, Garstang was convinced that the tumbled-down walls of Jericho evidenced the historical reliability of the biblical account in the book of Joshua.[14] Of course, he did not believe the walls were felled by the blare of the rams' horns, but most likely by an earthquake, a common phenomenon in the region. Twenty years later, Dame Kathleen Kenyon, director of the British School of

---

[12] This method that must be approached with caution. For example, the Palestinian village of al-Jib was identified by nineteenth-century American explorer Charles Robinson with ancient Gibeon, even though it may simply be preserving a Semitic word for hill (*gibah*). The linguistic connection was first made by French explorer Charles Claremont-Ganneau in 1870. It was later reinforced by the discovery of ostraca bearing the Hebrew letters *gzr*.

[13] For example, et-Tell/Bethsaida has been identified by its chief excavator, Rami Arav, as the biblical capital of the Geshurite kingdom (Deut 3:14; 2 Sam 3:3; 15:8) despite the lack of any reliable corroborating evidence. See Juha Pakkala, "What do we know about Geshur?" *JSOT* 24.2 (2010): 155-173.

[14] John Garstang, *The Foundations of Bible History: Joshua; Judges* (London, 1931).

Archaeology in Jerusalem, determined with scientific certainty based on more refined methodologies that the city walls Garstang believed were felled by Joshua at the end of the Late Bronze Age should be dated several centuries before Joshua— that is, to the Early Bronze Age. Efforts by Jewish and Christian to offer alternative dates for Joshua's putative conquest are thwarted by the temporal bookends of Egypt's 300-year occupation of Canaan on the one hand, and evidence (albeit scant) for pre-monarchical Israel on the other.[15]

In the Early Bronze Age II-III periods (3100-2300 BCE), many cities at the peak of prosperity, including Megiddo, experienced rapid systemic collapse. Several of these cities rebounded during the Middle Bronze period (2000-1600 BCE), along with the establishment of new settlements. Then, as mentioned in connection with Tel Megiddo, a second urban decline occurred just before the end of the Late Bronze Age (1200 BCE), this time more widely than before. Many theories attempting to account for these urban failures have been advanced over the years—famine, disease, conflict, and others—but it is generally accepted that it was due to no single cause. It is reasonable to assume that the waxing and waning of cities in the region has a lot to do with their location in and around the western tip of the Fertile Crescent, where cities and villages were most likely to experience the precarious interplay of factors related to climate change and geology, including intermittent famine, migration, invasion, plague, pestilence, and earthquakes.[16]

---

[15] Among the scant evidence is line 27 of the Merneptah victory stela, which recounts the victories of the Pharaoh Merneptah over various Canaanite city-states and refers to a people (not a city-state) called Israel. The stela, discovered in Thebes by Sir Flinders Petrie in 1896, and currently housed in the Egyptian Museum, Cairo, is securely dated to about 1207 BCE. See https://egypt-museum.com/victory-stele-of-merneptah/.

[16] See Marc Van De Mieroop, *A History of the Ancient Near East* (Hoboken, NJ: Wiley-Backwell, 2015); A. Mazar, "The Emergence of Cities: The Early Bronze Age (ca. 3300-2300 BCE)" in *Archaeology in the Land of the Bible* (New York City: Doubleday,

This second great collapse was followed by rapid settlement of the northern hill country in the vicinity of Samaria and Shechem (today's Palestinian Nablus) around the beginning of the Iron Age (1200–1000 BCE). At that time, various Canaanite tribes no longer economically tethered to the defunct urban systems on the plain, sought agricultural livelihoods away from marauding Sea Peoples like the Philistines, whose conquests led to the withdrawal of Egyptian administrative centers and garrisons from around Beth She'an, Megiddo, Lachish, and other major cities throughout Canaan.

The agrarian villages established by Canaanites in the hill country were products of intensive labor, beginning with the necessary digging of cisterns followed by the removal of rocks and boulders, leveling, and terracing for the construction of houses and pens and the cultivations of grains and trees. Settlers consisted of various Canaanite families, clans, and tribes, many of which would soon coalesce under the henotheistic influence of a Semitic priestly group who celebrated an escape from Egyptian bondage under a leader named Moses (an Egyptian name) to emerge into the light of history as a people called "Israel."[17] The unifying principle, apparently influenced by a Midian priest, remembered as Moses's father-in-law Jethro / Reuel, centered around a desert god designated by the letters Yahweh, whose alternative name, the plural Elohim, came to accommodate the chief deity (El) and polytheism of Canaanite tribes. This hypothesis for the emergence of a people called Israel is supported by the biblical narrative, which sets the Levites aside as the only tribe without its own geographical region but placing them in 48 priestly shrines scattered

---

1990), 91-150; and Raphael Greenberg, *Early Urbanizations in the Levant: A Regional Narrative* (London: Leicester University Press, 2002), 2-4.

[17] The historical origin of the name "Israel," which can mean "God contends," or "he who struggles with God," is unknown. Its earliest epigraphical mention is on the Merneptah victory stela, dated to ca. 1207 BCE. It is the name given to Jacob following his struggle with an angel, who states, "You shall no longer be called Jacob, but Israel, for you have contended with God and with men and have prevailed" (Gen. 32:28).

throughout the land, including the six Cities of Refuge (Num. 35:1-8).

According to field surveys, Canaanite/Israelite settlements in the IA I period ranged approximately seven to seventeen acres in size.[18] By about 1000 BCE, the start of the IA II period, growing populations, with their emerging ethnic identities and associations, led to the rise of capital cities in regional kingdoms in the southern Levant, including Ammon, Moab, Edom, Israel, and Judah. Despite their imposing size, IA II cities sheltered relatively few residents within their walls. Of course, the king (or governor) and priests, along with their families and servants would enjoy the protection of the city. Depending on its size and role, a city might also house an infantry regiment or a fleet of horse-drawn chariots. And then there were the officials charged with the inevitable collection of taxes from local farmers and herdsmen—in the currency of cereals, vegetables, and animals—who might expect to find refuge within the city in times of war in return for aiding its defense.

With the threat of Assyrian imperial expansion from the east, cities west of the Euphrates (called Abar-Nahara by the neo-Assyrians) began investing in the construction of defensive infrastructures to protect their palaces, temples, administrative buildings, water systems, storehouses, stables, residential structures, and barracks. They surrounded themselves with massively thick walls made of fine-cut ashlars, laid with precision in solid or casemate (chambered) construction; piled up earthen ramparts and slippery limestone slopes (glacis) to impede and deflect chariots and battering rams; and built strong bastions and high watchtowers alongside massive gate complexes that consisted of two, four, or even six chambers. But at the end of the day, none of these defensive structures were

---

[18] "Cities," *ABD*, I.1037-41. See also Nicolae Roddy, "Landscape of Shadows: The Image of City on the Hebrew Bible." Pp. 11-21 in Cities *Through the Looking Glass*, edited by R. Arav (Winona Lake, IN: Eisenbrauns, 2008); also, John W. Rogerson and John Vincent, *The City in Biblical Perspective* (London: Equinox 2009).

able to preserve their kingdoms against the voracious appetites of expanding empires and their mercenary armies.[19]

As mentioned above, one aspect of the Mesopotamian city is their close association with their patron gods. Jerusalem's relationship with its own divine patron is well attested in the earlier, triumphalist draft (Dtr[1]) of what would come to be known as the Deuteronomistic history; however, in the searing aftermath of Jerusalem's destruction, a radically new perspective emerges—namely, the prophetic condemnation of the city as a prostitute (*zonah*; Isa 1:21; Ezek 16:35-52) and city of blood (*'ir hadamim*; Ezek 22:2; 24:6), which helped provide an explanation for what had gone so terribly wrong that Yahweh would destroy his own city and house. This conviction was apparently easier to embrace than entertaining the notion that Babylon's Marduk was more powerful than Judah's national god, Yahweh.[20]

According to the prophetic perspective, the destruction of Jerusalem was directed by the hand of God in response to Judah's continued disobedience and lack of repentance. Ultimately, the responsibility for leading the nation in the right way falls to the king, and although Josiah was the biblical

---

[19] The literature on the archaeology of cities is extensive, but mostly site specific. For general overviews see "Fortifications (Levant)," in ABD 2. 844-45; W. Dever, "Archaeology, Urbanism, and the Rise of the Israelite State," in *Urbanism in Antiquity from Mesopotamia to Crete* (eds., W. E. Aufrecht, N. A. Mirau, and S. W. Gauley; JSOTSup 244; Sheffield: Sheffield Academic Press, 1997), 172-93; V. Fritz, *The City in Ancient Israel* (Sheffield: Sheffield Academic Press, 1995); I. Finkelstein, "The Great Transformation: The 'Conquest' of the Highland Frontiers and the Rise of the Territorial States," in *The Archaeology of Society in the Holy Land* (ed. T. Levy; London: Leicester University Press, 1995), 349-62; R. Gonen, "Urban Canaan in the Late Bronze Period," *BASOR* 253 (1984), 61-73; and F. S. Frick, *The City in Ancient Israel*, *SBLDS* 36 (Atlanta, GA: Scholars Press, 1977).

[20] The idea of a patron deity rejecting its city is not altogether unique in the ancient Near East. In a late-third millennium BCE epic, the fall of Akkad is interpreted in terms of divine displeasure with the city, for just as the Lord brings the Babylonians against Jerusalem for the "sins of Manasseh" (2 Kgs 23:26-27), the storm god Enlil brings the Gutians upon Akkad for the sins of king Naram-Sin, a move that compels Inanna (Ishtar) to abandon her temple and join the attackers in their assault. Millard C. Lind, *Yahweh is a Warrior* (Scottdale, PA: Herald Press, 1980), 110-11.

writer's favorite for promulgating the law of Moses throughout the land, apparently his virtue was not enough to mitigate the sins of his grandfather, Manasseh. King Manasseh ruled longer than any other Israelite monarch—fifty-five years, in fact—during which time he successfully negotiated his nation's survival under its Assyrian overlords; thus, it is difficult to fault him on historical grounds and accounts why the Bible is all but silent on these facts. At any rate, the biblical Judahites mistakenly placed their trust in their kings and in the fortified walls of their eternal capital (cf. 2 Chr 7:16; 2 Kgs 21:7), believing their nation would somehow be delivered from conquest. This misguided "Zion theology," which had persisted since Sennacherib's failure to breach King Hezekiah's city more than a century earlier (701 BCE.; 2 Kgs 18:13-19:37; Isa 36-37), continued to poison the minds of the leaders of Jeremiah's generation, including that of Pashur, chief officer of the temple (Jer 20:1-6). Jeremiah's prophecy regarding the certainty of Jerusalem's destruction as the product of divine wrath would become essential for the rise of Scripture, but it also casts a net implicating every city of the world. As failed repositories of unconscious trust, even the greatest and most fortified of cities cannot fulfill its promise of deliverance from destruction. The ruins of great cities all over the world bear silent witness to this reality.

The City in the Hebrew Bible

What might it mean that the first biblical city is founded by Cain, a fratricide-in-exile (Gen 4:17) whose sedentary life as an agriculturalist is disrupted by a fit of searing anger (*wayyihar me'od*) toward his pastoralist brother for whom the Lord shows favor? Forced into exile by the Lord's curse of the ground upon which his lifestyle depends, Cain abandons his sedentary way of life, but ironically ends up inaugurating the most rooted mode of human existence—namely, the city—as if somehow to regain his permanent hold upon the earth. The fixed settlement he builds is an artificial creation, an enduring legacy named after

his son, Enoch.[21] Enoch City is ruled by Lemek, whose name is
a play on the word *melek* (king) through metathesis, thus making
a literary connection between the institutions of monarchy and
fortified cities.[22]

Cain's apparent inability or lack of will to prevail against sin
(*hata*) "crouching at his door" (Gen 4:7) alienates him from God
and fellow human beings, leaving the reader with a sense of
lonely abandonment from the warmth of human relationship.
Something of Cain's isolation finds itself transmitted through his
son Enoch into the very DNA of the city, or as Tarazi observes,
"turning God's gift of flesh into one of stone."[23] Although Cain's
progeny disappears with the Flood, the city and its related
technologies live on in trades of building and toolmaking
(4:20–22), and estrangement from God and other human beings
resumes in the lineage of Noah's son Ham and his grandson,
Canaan (9:20-27), the eponymous ancestor of the land of great
cities like Tyre and Sidon, Hazor, and Megiddo.

By contrast, the pastoral life of Abel is resumed in the *toledot* of
Seth (4:25), whose children are ever at home navigating the
natural terrain in search of grass and grains, untethered to the
land but for temporary sojourns at life-giving oases, God's gift
to the wilderness. With the birth of Seth's son Enosh, human
beings begin to "call upon the name of the Lord" (v. 26),
unsurprising to anyone who has spent time in the open
wilderness free of artificial distraction, rich in the beauty of
creation, and most amenable to an encounter with the living
God.[24] A few generations later, the Sethite Enoch "walks with
God and is no more because God takes him" (5:24).

---

[21] This Enoch is not to be confused with the son of Jared and father of Methuselah,
who "walked with God and was not, for God took him" (Gen 5:22-24).

[22] Metathesis refers to the transposition of letters or sounds, as in the story of Babel,
associated by the storyteller with *balal*, meaning "confusion."

[23] *TROS*, 151-58.

[24] See Robert D. Miller, *Yahweh: Origin of a Desert God* (Göttingen: Vandenhoeck &
Ruprecht, 2021).

The story of the city of Babel and its monumental tower marks the antediluvian apex of human technological achievement. Its name plays on the Akkadian word for gate (*bab*; *bab*-ilani, gate of the gods) and the Hebrew word for confusion (*balal*, another example of metathesis). Originally, the story was almost certainly inspired by the famous Etemenanki ziggurat of Babylon, the ruins of which lie approximately 60 miles south of present-day Baghdad. The structure, which had been destroyed and rebuilt many times over millennia, must have been impressive in the eyes of the sixth-century BCE exiles. Its upper platform was considered the meeting point between heaven and earth, allowing Babylon's priestly astronomers to chart the nighttime sky and interpret astrological portents and divine omens.

According to the biblical story, the Lord looks down from the skies and sees mortals conspiring to achieve something that would allow them fully to unite and transgress the boundary between divine and human realms. Their efforts call to mind the function of the angel (*hakkerubim*) with the flaming sword, who guards the way to the Tree of Life (Gen 3:22-24), thus preventing humans from reentering Paradise with their special knowledge and to "be as gods." Observing their progress, the Lord intervenes. He diversifies their common language and scatters them abroad, leaving behind a fitting monument to humankind's proud, foolish, and failed ambition.

Following the great deluge, cities and city-states[25] still continue to be associated with bellicose warriors and outcasts. Upon planting the world's first vineyard, a sedentary industry of which Cain would likely approve, Noah passes out drunk and naked in his tent, setting the scene for Ham's indiscretion and subsequent curse upon Canaan and his descendants, many of

---

[25] Simply put, the essential difference between a city and a city-state is that the former is an urban settlement withing a larger polity, while the latter is autonomous.

which are eponymous founders of great Mesopotamian and Egyptian cities and city-states.

> Egypt became the father of Ludim, Anamim, Lehabim, Naphtuhim, Pathrusim, Casluhim, and Caphtorim, from which the Philistines come. Canaan became the father of Sidon his firstborn, and Heth, and the Jebusites, the Amorites, the Girgashites, the Hivites, the Arkites, the Sinites, the Arvadites, the Zemarites, and the Hamathites. Afterward the families of the Canaanites spread abroad. And the territory of the Canaanites extended from Sidon, in the direction of Gerar, as far as Gaza, and in the direction of Sodom, Gomorrah, Admah, and Zeboiim, as far as Lasha. (Gen 10:10-19)[26]

The negative portrayal of the city continues throughout the remainder of the Torah and into the Prophets. In Genesis 19, the wicked cities of Sodom and Gomorrah are destroyed for their extreme lawlessness and violence. Before this, we see Lot "sitting at the gates of Sodom" (19:1), where only judges and other persons would be seated, which indicates he was not standing and moving through the crowd as an ordinary citizen would be doing, in contrast to Abraham, who sits at the entrance of his tent out in the wilderness, far away from urban society.[27] Likewise, Gibeah, an Israelite city of the tribe of Benjamin, is not only remembered as the city from which Saul reigns (1 Sam 10:26; 22:6; 23:19), but also for the brutal rape and murder of a Levite's concubine (Judges 19). The trouble with cities is not only that they are arenas of violence and injustice, but that people continue investing trust in them for the things they are expected to deliver most, namely, security and deliverance from the ills of the world. This view appears to originate in the schools of eighth-century BCE anti-establishment prophetic figures like Amos and Hosea, who

---

[26] The first-century historian Flavius Josephus associates the Egyptian names listed above with cities apparently lost to history in the Ethiopic War during the 15th century BCE (*Ant.* 1.6).

[27] Raymond Harari, "Abraham's Nephew Lot: A Biblical Portrait," *Tradition: A Journal of Orthodox Jewish Thought* 25. 1 (1989): 31-41, (https://www.jstor.org/stable/23260604).

viewed cities as places where justice no longer obtained and idolatry flourished, sanctioned by both king and priest.[28] Their message is reinforced and reapplied in prophetic judgments against Jerusalem nearly a century and a half later.

The biblical critique of fortified cities is levelled especially against Samaria and Jerusalem—capital cities whose inability to remain in faithful obedience to the Heavenly King and Shepherd left them and the rest of their nations vulnerable, bereft of any hope for divine protection in the face of the advancing threat of great empires. In powerfully graphic imagery, Samaria is labelled a prostitute for her adultery (read idolatry) and disregard for prophetic justice and righteousness. Jerusalem is even more contemptible in having learned nothing from the example of her elder sister (cf. Ezek 16:46-52; 23:1-49). How much more might these examples of impotency, artificiality, and impermanence of so-called "holy cities" offer modern cities standing atop millennia of human debris, arrogantly and erroneously imagining that they will endure forever? As Qoheleth observes, "There is no remembrance of past things, nor will people yet to come be remembered by those who follow after them" (Eccl.1:11).

As we have seen, the prophetic critique of cities as repositories of idolatrous, misplaced trust includes a condemnation of ills associated with idolatry, most notably the lack of justice within their gates. The eighth-century BCE prophet Amos is especially notable for calling out socioeconomic injustice against a society that fails to realize, let alone address its own culpability. He levels oracles of doom against a wider circle of powerful cities of the Levant, including Damascus of Aram (Syria); Phoenician Tyre; the Philistine cities of Gaza, Ashdod, and Ekron; Edom's Teman and Bozra; Rabbah of the Ammonites; Jerusalem; and finally, Samaria, capital of the northern kingdom of Israel,

---

[28] Although treated in each their own chapters in this volume, the Bible's negative regard for cities and its critique of kings and cult are inextricably related; see *TROS*, 153-58.

which is sustained throughout the rest of the book. Recurring lines in the international oracles include the formulaic "For three transgressions and for four, I will not revoke the punishment," indicating the kingdoms and city-states have not only attained but have gone well beyond the maximum level of wickedness that would justify the Lord's judgment against it; thus, he will send a fire upon the city walls that shall devour all its fortifications (1:4, 7, 10, 12, 14; 2:2, 5).

God's judgment against the city of Samaria includes a word for the king, Jeroboam II, whose power and influence extends outward through the network of formerly Levitical cities like Bethel, Dan, Gilgal, Carmel, and others, all of which had been converted to a network of state-supporting shrines by Jeroboam I (1 Kgs 12:25-33; Amos 7:13). The system sanctions the exploitation of herders and landowners—a demographic to which Amos himself likely belonged (7:14)—by elite members of Israelite society who were able to direct ill-gotten wealth to their own coffers. At a time of perceived economic prosperity occurring during a temporary respite from the looming threat of Assyria, Amos boldly asserts the inevitable destruction of Israel and the demise of its leadership, proclaiming "Jeroboam will die by the sword and Israel must go into exile away from his land" (7:11). Amos's judgment against the king and cities of Israel indicates their interconnectedness. His words are fulfilled when they together meet their end at the hands of the Assyrians just a few decades later.

An important aspect of Amos's critique of the city is its arrogant misplaced confidence in its monumental fortifications. Armed with the word of the Lord, Amos proclaims, "I abhor the pride of Jacob and hate his citadels; and I will deliver up the city and all that is in it" (6:8), adding that those hoping to seek refuge within it will be "dragged away with grappling hooks through breaches in the city wall" (4:2-3). According to Amos, such fortifications offer no refuge, for the God of Creation will surely destroy them:

> The one who made the Pleiades and Orion,
> and turns deep darkness into the morning,
> and darkens the day into night,
> Who calls for the waters of the sea,
> and pours them out on the surface of the earth,
> the Lord is his name,
> who makes destruction flash out against the strong,
> so that destruction comes upon the fortress. (5:4-5)

To be sure, the ruined foundations of city walls, gates, and bastions toppled during the Age of Empires, with the help of a few major earthquakes, are still visible throughout the Levant, serving as humbled silent witnesses to the impermanence of all human achievement.

The prophet Hosea, a somewhat later contemporary of Amos, employs a great deal of rural imagery but is no less critical of Israel's cities. Gilead and Adam, as examples, are lawless and violent; they defile the nation with blood (Hos 6:7-10). In decrying the fact that Israel has "forgotten his Maker," Hosea establishes a mutually exclusive correlation between building cities and "remembering" the Lord in trust and obedience:

> Israel has forgotten his Maker and built citadels,
> and Judah has multiplied its fortified cities;
> But I will send a fire upon all their cities,
> and it shall devour all their strongholds. (Hos 8:14)

Like Amos, Hosea asserts that fortified cities offer only illusory hope for protection against the Lord, who raises up enemies against them in judgment.[29]

The word of God through the lips of Amos and Hosea have been vindicated by history. The kingdom of Israel was shaken by at least one great earthquake (ca. 760 BCE), followed by the

---

[29] For more in-depth coverage on the book of Hosea, see Richard Benton, *Hosea: A Commentary* (St. Paul, MN: OCABS Press, 2021).

destructive conquest of the Assyrian Tiglath-Pileser III (biblical Pul); the subsequent siege and deportations carried out by Shalmanesar V; and the decisive fall of Samaria to Sargon II in 722 BCE, all of which contributed to bringing the history of the northern kingdom to an end. Roughly a century and a half later, the kingdom of Judah would fare no better. Whether the disaster is a natural one, or the result of belligerent nations, trusting in cities for security and defense is an ultimately futile endeavor. The expectation that the fortified city, with its massive walls, deflecting ramps, and towering bastions, would offer the highest and best defense against an enemy was shown in hindsight to be of no avail against the mighty arm of God. A mindless and rebellious people who forgets its Maker and shirks its obligation to uphold justice and righteousness will be cast out into exile away from its familiar streets.

A later contemporary of Amos, Micah of Moresheth, also rails against the socioeconomic disparities resulting from the development of robust structures of centralized wealth and power. From his rural village in the Judean foothills (Shephelah), the prophet boldly decries the abuses of power sanctioned by the royal and priestly elites of Samaria and Jerusalem. Extolling Yahweh's anger, Micah proclaims that God himself will personally uproot these centers of national iniquity and return the hills they shamelessly occupy to natural, agricultural uses:

> For lo, the Lord is coming out of his place,
>   and will come down and tread upon the high places of the earth.
> Then the mountains will melt under him
>   and the valleys will burst open,
> like wax near the fire,
> like waters poured down a steep place.
> All this is for the transgression of Jacob
> and for the sins of the house of Israel.
> What is the transgression of Jacob?
> Is it not Samaria?
> And what are the high places of Judah?

Are they not Jerusalem?
Therefore I will make Samaria a heap in the open country,
a place for planting vineyards.
I will pour down her stones into the valley,
and uncover her foundations. (Micah 1:3-6)

It is clear the governing structures rooted in the capital cities sanction the actions that unjustly remove land and property from powerless tenants of the land:

They covet fields, and seize them;
houses, and take them away;
they oppress householder and house,
people and their inheritance. (Micah 2:1-2)

For the eighth-century BCE prophets, the city is less a place for seeking refuge than it is a place where wickedness thrives. The greater the city, the more it exposes itself as a target for a judgment it cannot withstand.

Yet another prophetic assault on the city is leveled in the book of Zephaniah, a book that is difficult to date in that it has endured much editing over time; however, the prophet's warning against ultimate reliance upon the city remains clear and timeless. Samaria and Jerusalem—or any major city, for that matter—remain unsustainable, artificial constructions casting shadows of social and economic injustice upon the earth.

Ah, soiled, defiled, oppressing city!
It listens to no voice;
It accepts no correction.
It does not trust in the LORD;
It does not draw near to its God. (Zeph 3:1-2)

Echoing Amos's words against Samaria concerning the fearsome "day of the Lord," Zephaniah foretells a day of devastation against the fortified cities (1:15-16). Zephaniah's taunts Jerusalem's air of arrogance and self-sufficiency, which will bring about its own destruction, returning the fortified city to its natural state:

Is this the exultant city
that lived secure,
that said to itself,
"I am, and there is no one else"?
What a desolation it has become,
a lair for wild animals?
Everyone who passes by it
hisses and shakes the fist. (2:15)

In the final years of the eighth century BCE, Isaiah ben Amoz, court prophet and priest in service to kings Ahaz and Hezekiah, begins railing against the pride of Judah's cities and the false promises of security they offer. The fact that Isaiah is a Jerusalemite priest of the Aaronid-Zadokite line and apparently a court official makes his case as a critical insider all the more extraordinary. What crisis inspired this priest to prophesy? Perhaps the still-smoldering Assyrian destruction of Samaria helped him to realize that Israel's fortified cities were failed repositories of hope for deliverance; for as Sennacherib and his Assyrian forces pressed southward, Isaiah begins echoing his northern counterparts, proclaiming "your strong cities will be like the deserted places of the Hivites and the Amorites . . . and there will be desolation; for you have forgotten the God of your salvation" (Isa 17:9-10). Like the cities of the newly fallen kingdom of Israel, Judah's cities are unable to strand against the Lord's impending judgment.

Other Judahite prophets would continue building on the prophetical convictions of the mid- to late-eighth century BCE, which they came to apply full-force to their own social and political situations. The so-called Isaiah apocalypse (chs. 24-27), which is likely a reworked oracle formerly directed at Israel, now becomes a powerful anti-establishment diatribe aimed at Judah's reckless leaders, proclaiming an enigmatic judgment in rural metaphor:

The city of chaos (*tohu*) is broken down,
every house is shut up so that none can enter.
There is a cry for wine in the streets,

all joy has gone dark,
and gladness has fled from the land,
Desolation remains in the city,
whose gates are smashed to ruins.
For thus it shall be on the earth and among the nations,
like the shaking of an olive tree,
or the gleaning of grapes at harvest season. (Isa 24:10-13)

Roughly a century after the Assyrian siege of Jerusalem, Ezekiel extols Jerusalem's inevitable destruction from exile in Babylon. In 597 BCE, King Nebuchadnezzar of Babylon had attacked Jerusalem and carried young King Jehoiachin, the Queen Mother, and members of Jerusalem's elite society, including Ezekiel, an official priest of the Aaronid-Zadokite line. As Ezekiel sat along the Chebar channel, a tributary of the river Euphrates, "the heavens opened" and he saw "visions of God" (*mar'ot elohim*), thus inaugurating his career as a prophet. The book named for him warns against the insidious dangers of prophets who "whitewash the truth"[30] with erroneous assertions that God would spare the nation from destruction and that one could find refuge within its walled cities (Ezek 13:3-16). Nowhere is the prophetic indictment against cities more forcefully delivered than in Ezekiel's indictment against Jerusalem, which he calls a "whore" (16:35-52) and "city of blood" (22:2; 24:6). His bizarre sign-act of cutting hairs from his head and beard carries a sign of what is about to transpire in Jerusalem.

Thus says the Lord God: This is Jerusalem; I have set her in the center of the nations, with countries all around her. But she has rebelled against my judgments [*mishpatim*] and my statutes [*huqqot*], becoming more wicked than the nations and the countries all around her, rejecting my laws and not following my statutes. Therefore, thus says the Lord God: Because you have multiplied transgressions [*hamanekem*] more than the nations that are all around you and have not followed my statutes or kept my

---

[30] The term used here refers to plastering with *taphel*, an inferior mortar made of clay, instead of the more durable slaked lime (calcium hydroxide).

> judgments but have acted according to the judgments of the
> nations all around you; therefore, thus says the Lord God: I, I
> myself, am coming against you; I will execute judgments among
> you in the sight of the nations. (Ezek 5:5-8)

In the end, Ezekiel asserts that Jerusalem's sins are far more
grievous than those of Sodom and Gomorrah in that it had
learned nothing from the example of their destruction, let alone
from the more recent destruction of her sister, Samaria. How
then can anyone expect to take refuge there? How will anyone
survive the inevitable destruction of Yahweh's judgment? If the
fortified city cannot stand, where is one to find safety? It is here
that Ezekiel introduces the entrance of the New Jerusalem, the
otherworldly counterpart of the failed city in which God dwells
with the righteous. This concept continues in the books of
Zechariah, Isaiah, and others, including the NT Apocalypse's
Heavenly City.

As Ezekiel extols Jerusalem's inevitable destruction from
Babylon roughly 550 miles toward the east (in modern-day
Iraq), his contemporary, the prophet Jeremiah, warns of a
similar outcome from within Jerusalem's fortified walls. As a
descendant of the northern Levitical priestly tradition, Jeremiah
brings his foreboding message to Jerusalem from the fields of
Anatoth, a tiny settlement located a few miles northeast of
Jerusalem, to which Solomon had exiled David's faithful high
priest, Abiathar (1 Kgs 2:26). Despite having different
perspectives on the predicament at hand, both are in full accord
that the Lord has slated Jerusalem for irrevocable and imminent
destruction. However, Jeremiah is forbidden to intercede on
Jerusalem's behalf (Jer 14:11-12; cf. 7:16, 11:14, 15:1) and
proclaims there will be no refuge within its walls
(Jer 23:17; 27:9-10).

> The Lord said to me: Do not pray on behalf of this people. When
> they fast, I do not hear their cry, and although they offer burnt
> offering and offerings of grain, I do not accept them. But I will
> consume them by the sword, by famine, and by pestilence. Then
> I said, "Ah, Lord God! Here are [false] prophets saying to them,

'You shall not see the sword, nor shall you have famine, but I will give you true peace in this place.'" (Jer 14:11-12)

The passage shows that Jeremiah must combat false prophets who had been poisoned by the obsolete "Zion theology" left over from Yahweh's celebrated defense of Jerusalem against the Assyrian siege roughly a century earlier (Isa 37:35). Jeremiah rails against the "false pen of the scribes," who proclaim their misguided assurances of a new round of divine deliverance, failing to recognize that imminent divine judgment applies to them (8:8). One such lying prophet, Hananiah from Gibeon, confronts Jeremiah publicly in the temple, proclaiming an oracular outcome without basis in fact—thus making clear why it is the Bible lacks a book of Hananiah. Hananiah prophesies falsely:

> "Thus says the Lord of hosts, the God of Israel, I have broken the yoke of the king of Babylon. Within two years I will bring back to this place all the vessels of the Lord's house, which King Nebuchadnezzar of Babylon took away from this place and carried to Babylon. I will also bring back to this place King Jeconiah [Jehoiachin], son of Jehoiachim of Judah, and all the exiles from Judah who went to Babylon, says the Lord, for I will break the yoke of the king of Babylon." (28:2-4)

Jeremiah, however, proclaims the imminent judgment of the Lord against Jerusalem, and taunts those who would seek refuge in the city as they did in Hezekiah's day (8:14). No longer can Judah entreat the Lord for protection from its enemies, for the Babylonian empire and its mercenaries are the very instruments God is bringing against them and no city can save them.

> They shall destroy with the sword your fortified cities
> in which you trust. (5:15-17)

All too late, only the ruins of the city reveal the ultimate refuge:

> For you, O Lord, have made the city a heap, the fortified city a ruin,[. . .]For you, O Lord, have been a citadel for the poor, a fortification to the needy in their distress, a refuge [*machseh*] from the storm, and shade from the heat. (Isa 25:2-4)

As with every object of the prophetic critique, the human city has an ultimate divine counterpart, an invincible fortified city accessible only through the prophetic word:

> For indeed I have made you this day a fortified city, an iron pillar, and bronze wall, against all the land, against the kings of Judah, against its princes, against its priests, and against the people of the land. And they will fight against you, but they shall not prevail against you, for I am with you, says the Lord, to deliver you. (Jer 1:18-19)

Conclusion

Early migratory hunters and pastoralists coming upon a Sumerian city-state for the first time must surely have been awestruck, perhaps suspicious of such grand artificiality imposed against the backdrop of the natural landscape, while those accustomed to dwelling in and around the city would likely have enjoyed a sense of familiarity and security. Did the former really expect that gods were dwelling within the walls of the city and in houses specially built for them? Did they remember the place where divinity appears in full force and without mediation—out in the desert, away from the city and its heart of stone? Whatever power and majesty these monuments may have exerted over the ancients, the prophetically influenced priestly scribes were unimpressed. They were able to imagine that a Jerusalem in ruins—and by extension all cities—could revert to a living wilderness, a home for jackals (Jer 9:11).

Such is the motivation that drives the prophetically influenced writers of the Bible to level a decidedly negative view of fortified cities, extolling their fleeting existence founded upon the wickedness they harbor—most notably, idolatry and social injustice, but also foolish pride and arrogance in their presentation as impenetrable bastions of security. The prophetic indictment makes clear that any investment of trust in fortified cities is misplaced, and that the only inviolable refuge is obedience to the Word of God, a word proclaimed through the speech and actions of true prophets (past and present) who hold the conviction that the welfare of the city depends upon social and economic justice and not on concrete and steel.

Cities today are experiencing a diminished ability to provide the security and well-being people expect of them. Built by paid laborers instead of slaves, they still rank among humanity's greatest achievements, but instead of marauding hordes, modern challenges include maintaining sufficient resources to accommodate their burgeoning populations; acquiring affordable alternatives to non-renewable energy sources,[31] and bridging the great divide in wealth disparity to provide food for the hungry, homes for the homeless, and jobs for the jobless, food for the hungry, and so on—will greatly diminish. Until the end, our attitude toward cities should be tempered by the wisdom of Qoheleth, who observes:

> I made great works; I built houses and planted vineyards for myself. I made myself gardens and parks and planted in them all kinds of fruit trees. I made myself pools from which to water the forest of growing trees. I bought male and female slaves and had slaves that were born in my house; I also had great possessions of herds and flocks, more than any that had been before me in Jerusalem. I also gathered for myself silver and gold and the treasure of kings . . . then I considered all that my hands had done and the toil I had spent doing it, and again, all was vanity and a chasing after wind, and there was nothing to be gained under the sun. (Eccl 2:4-8a, 11).

---

[31] See Ashley Dawson, *Extreme Cities: The Peril and Promise of Urban Life in the Age of Climate Change* (New York: Verso, 2017). Reliable sources such as the MIT Climate Portal suggest that cities today are responsible for anywhere from 50 to 80 percent of all global GHG emissions. See https://climate.mit.edu/explainers/cities-and-climate-change.

Chapter 4
The Trouble with Chariots

A king is not saved by a great army; a warrior is not saved by his strength. A horse is a vain hope for safety, for it cannot deliver by its might. (Ps 33:16-17)

Because you trust in your own way, in the multitude of your mighty men; a tumult shall rise among your people, and all your fortresses shall be plundered. (Hos 10:13-14)

Apart from its own fortified walls, an ancient city-state's highest and best line of defense was its armada of metal-clad, two-wheeled, horse-drawn chariots, with drivers and archers, charging ahead of thousands of fleet-footed infantry troops scurrying to keep up with them. Although the deployment of war chariots eventually gave way to horses bred specially for speed and versatility, the chariot remains a potent symbol of military strength and security in the literary imagination well beyond its use. By contrast, the prophetically influenced priestly scribes who struggled to make sense of the destruction of Jerusalem held a much different point of view. They maintained that Israel had forgotten its Protector and trusted in its own hands; thus they were left defenseless against the Babylonian onslaught that God had brought upon the nation. From the advantage of hindsight, they decided that a kingdom's highest and best line of defense was never to be found in iron chariots, but in chariots and horses of fire (*rekeb 'esh ve-sus 'esh*) representing the line of true prophets from Moses through the succession narrative of Elijah and Elisha, and on to the "prophet like me" (Deut 18:15) in the writer's own time, likely referring to Jeremiah.

The localized conflicts of the ancient world are nothing like the perils that threaten the world today. The investment of vast amounts of wealth and trust in today's advanced weaponry—nuclear missiles, M1-series Abrams tanks, F-35 fighter jets, and so on—would seem to call for serious reflection on our nation's dependency upon them. The notion that having the largest stockpile of weapons can save a nation simply by making it feel safe, whole, justified may be dangerously misguided. Ironically, the size of a nation's military stockpile may be less a measure of its strength and security than its degree of fear and insecurity (albeit difficult to quantify). If so, what might that mean for the United States, given it is the greatest military spender in the world? According to the National Priorities Project, U.S. defense expenditures recently exceeded $730 billion—roughly 64.5 percent of all federal discretionary spending. If one includes additional spending for related items not covered in this figure—such as veterans' affairs, homeland security, military law enforcement and incarceration, and so on—it would increase the total to over a trillion dollars. In fact, U.S. militarized spending exceeds the combined budgets of the next ten highest nations, including China, Russia, and Saudi Arabia.[1]

The fears and insecurities of the nation that fuel the unfettered growth of the nation's military-industrial monstrosity are further exploited and manipulated by a relatively small number of wealthy corporate elites in pursuit of greater personal wealth and power.[2] These captains of destructive industry are aided by the politicians and government officials they lobby and reward. Few Americans would deny the need for practical defense structures, but our culture of massive social insecurity and the

---

[1] National Priorities Project, "The Militarized Budget 2020." June 20, 2020; https://www.nationalpriorities.org/analysis/2020/militarized-budget-2020/. The data are derived from NATO through the Stockholm International Peace Research Institute (SIPRI).

[2] One wonders what would become of corporations like Lockheed-Martin, Northrop Grumman, Boeing, and others if world affairs would come to be managed strategically through economic strength instead of unlimited firepower. Roughly half of all military spending goes to private military contractors and their CEOs, while the healthcare needs of veterans whose alarming suicide rates continue to rise goes relatively unaddressed. The current Department of Defense Annual Suicide Report states the suicide rate for the active component of the US military in 2018 was 24.8 suicides per 100,000, having increased steadily from 18.5 per 100,000 in 2013. Archived in print digital format at https://www.dspo.mil.

people who stoke it and reap from it has resulted in a gargantuan stockpile of surplus weaponry at the hands of leaders lacking the wisdom for its safe and effective management. As a result, military and corporate access to this bloated, ready arsenal has led to the deaths of hundreds of thousands of innocent civilians around the world, either directly or by proxy. Outdated weaponry cast aside to make room for newer technology often finds its way into the hands of foreign governments and domestic urban police departments lacking adequate training or measured restraint in their use. In sum, the ongoing development and rampant stockpiling of the world's most dangerous conventional and nuclear weaponry leads one to wonder what it would take for the U.S. to live up to its vain motto "In God we trust." The prophetic perspective, best revealed when set against the role of war chariotry in the actual history and archaeology of the Levant, offers a realistic faith solution to the problem of today's dependency on world-destroying weapons of war.

Chariots in the Ancient World

Sometime around 3000 BCE, two- and four-wheeled wooden conveyances drawn by donkeys, mules, or oxen could be seen carting around everything from cabbages to kings. Over the centuries, horses were harnessed to new vehicular designs that permitted greater maneuverability, durability, and speed, qualities suitable for warfare. Israel, Judah, Ammon, Moab, and Edom, the relatively small Iron Age kingdoms sandwiched between the narrow rift between the Mediterranean Sea and the Arabian desert in the shifting buffer zone between meddlesome Egypt and the relentless kingdoms of northwestern Asia and Mesopotamia valued their chariot fleets. These were sources of pride and assurance in times of peace and stability, but with the advance of restless empires from the north and east, their chariots supplied a desperate last hope.[3]

It is not known how many chariots these ancient Levantine kingdoms possessed. Numbers in ancient sources like the Bible are simply not to be trusted. For example, according to 1 Samuel 13, the Philistine advance upward from the coast into the Israelite hill country included 30,000 chariots (*rekeb*) and 6,000 horsemen (*parashim*), while according to 1 Chr 19:7, a coalition of Ammonites and Aramean forces attacked Israel from the opposite direction with 32,000 chariots and 33,000 infantrymen (*ragli*). These numbers are clearly inflated to absurdity when one considers that one of the greatest battles ever recorded in ancient Near Eastern history—the 13th century BCE battle of Qadesh—involved only an estimated 2,000 to 3,000 chariots on each side.[4] Thutmose III's battle reliefs at Karnak record the taking of only 924 chariots as booty from the battle with Megiddo, and estimates are that neither side commanded hardly more than a thousand chariots.[5]

It is reasonable to assume that petty kingdoms like Israel and Judah possessed at least a few hundred to maybe a thousand plated chariots (*rekeb barzel*), a requisite number of horsemen (*parashim*), and perhaps a few battalions of foot soldiers (*ragli*). However, despite the many battles recounted throughout the Deuteronomistic history, no real accounting of them is given. In the earlier, Josianic-period draft of the Deuteronomistic history (Dtr[1]), numbers are triumphalist exaggerations. For example, "Solomon had 40,000 stalls of horses for his chariots"

---

[3] Nicolae Roddy, "Chariots of Fire, Unassailable Cities, and the One True King: The Prophetically Influenced Scribal Perspective on War." In *Orthodox Christian Perspectives on War*, edited by P. T. Hamalis and V. A. Karras, 61-84. (Notre Dame, IN: University of Notre Dame University Press, 2017). It should be noted that iron chariots were not actually made of iron, but of wood plated with bronze or iron.

[4] The battle was fought between Ramesses II and Muwatalli of Hatti, both of whom claimed to have won. See Mark Healy, *Qadesh 1300 B.C.: Clash of the Warrior Kings* (New York: Osprey, 1993).

[5] Eric Cline, *The Battles of Armageddon: Megiddo, and the Battles of the Jezreel Valley from the Bronze Age to the Nuclear Age* (Ann Arbor: The University of Michigan Press, 2000), 21.

(1 Kgs 4:26);[6] however, the post-destruction version (Dtr[2]) ignores such hyperbole, at least for Judah. There is relatively little mention of how many chariots and horses King David possessed, but he is said to have captured 1,700 chariot teams and 20,000 infantrymen from Aramaean king Hadadezer of Zobah in a single battle (2 Sam 8:3; 1 Chr 18:4) so presumably had them at his disposal. Again, the figures are hyperbolic, unreliable products of a triumphalist account of Judah's kings culminating in Josiah.

As discussed in Chapter Two, there is no extra-biblical evidence for the existence of a Davidic-Solomonic kingdom reaching anywhere close to the magnitude described in the Bible. If the Tel Dan inscription mentioned there does in fact refer to a Davidic dynasty, the eponymous founder is all but missing elsewhere in the historical record and was probably no more than a tribal leader whose dating cannot be known. The inscription recounts an invasion from the south by "thousands of chariots and thousands of horsemen" from the south, which hint at the existence of Israelite chariots in the mid-ninth century BCE, at which time Omri fortifies Samaria, consolidates his kingdom, and conquers territories beyond its borders. Omri is well evidenced historically as a major international player, while David and Solomon are not. However, because he is a northern king, he is mentioned only in passing in the biblical account of kings (1 Kgs 16:23-28; *cf* Mic 6:16).

Omri doubtlessly relied on chariots and horsemen to advance the boundaries of Israel across the Jordan river. The famous Kurkh monolith, an Assyrian inscription witnessing to the first six years of Shalmaneser III's campaign in Aram (Syria), briefly records the Assyrian leader's defeat at the Battle of Qarqar in 853 BCE. The stela mentions Ahab, king of Israel (reigned ca. 870-853 BCE), who joined King Hadadezer of Damascus in

---

[6] 2 Chr 9:25 puts the number 4,000, which has led some translators to assume a mistake in which "arbaim" (forty) was mistaken for "arba" (four).

leading a twelve-nation coalition that managed to stall the Assyrian advance for a three or four battle seasons.[7] Understandably, Shalmaneser III does not explicitly admit defeat, but the fact that the Assyrians were unable to make any significant progress westward for the next few years attests to the relative success of the coalition's campaign against them.[8] Important for our purposes is the Assyrian claim that Ahab of Israel had contributed 2,000 chariots of iron and 10,000 infantrymen to the opposing coalition, which was more than half the total of all allied resources combined and forty percent larger than Hadadezer's contribution. Although these numbers have not gone unchallenged and must remain suspect, the fact that the coalition succeeded in halting the Assyrian advance strongly supports the assertion that Israel and its allies possessed a well-equipped fighting force.

It is worth noting that the Bible is strangely silent about Ahab's glorious campaign. Any victories accorded to Ahab are the result of Yahweh's will and not Ahab's might. Even with the omission of this victory, the Bible's wicked king still gets plenty of press on account of his wife Jezebel's 450 prophets of Baal, their seizure of Naboth's ancestral vineyard (1 Kgs 21:1-16), and their relentless pursuit of the prophet Elijah. However, the Bible writer encourages readers interested in learning more about kings Ahab and Omri to consult the Annals of the Kings of Israel. Of course, these royal chronicles did not survive—and for good reason. They lavished praise upon Israel's kings, while the biblical account survives with its assertion that a nation cannot defend itself against the army of its own God. The prophetic perspective is that Israel should not have continued to rely on its chariots of iron, but upon the chariots of fire and horses of fire (*rekeb 'esh ve-sus 'esh*) of the Lord their God.

---

[7] Apparently a round number, as only eleven kings are actually listed.

[8] The Assyrian empire was eventually successful in establishing dominance in the Levant, as shown in on the famous Black Obelisk, on display in the British Museum, in which King Jehu of Israel is depicted in bas-relief bearing tribute to the Assyrian king, ca. 840 BCE.

Chariots in the Bible

The Bible has much to say about iron chariots (*rekeb barzel*), horsemen (*parashim*), and infantry (*ragli*). It is appropriate to think of biblical armies as pawns within a larger literary agenda aimed at magnifying the Lord's sovereignty over all the nations of the earth. As the King of Kings ruling with justice and righteousness (*mishpat ve-tzedakah*), God makes use of the arsenals of various kingdoms to bring about fulfillment of the divine purpose. It is significant that the number of Israelite chariots is relatively underrepresented compared to the greatly exaggerated resources of its enemies. The difference is apparent in both the Deuteronomistic history and in Chronicles, although each with a different purpose in mind. The former uses the numerical imbalance to posit defeat as a consequence for unrelenting disobedience; the latter, a post-exilic writer of the Persian period, emphasizes the Lord's willingness to fight on behalf of Israel when king and the nation are deserving of it, acknowledging often they were not. In both cases, enemy chariots are instruments in the hands of God, the just King and Warrior, who sets forth a universal standard which all nations must observe.

Besides the Philistine and Aramean battles mentioned earlier, Israel's other enemies have robust military resources as well. Egypt dispatches a host of chariots and horsemen in honor of Jacob's burial (Gen 50:9), while the Pharaoh who "does not know Joseph" (Exod 1:8) pursues Moses and the Hebrews with six hundred choice chariots (*rekeb bahur*) and an unspecified host of regular war chariots (Exod 14:6-7). Furthermore, Egyptian chariots and horses continue to be a great temptation for Israel throughout the Former Prophets. Solomon could purchase a chariot for 600 shekels and a horse for 250 shekels and broker them profitably to the kings of Hatti and Aram (1 Kgs 10:29). However, a stern warning against relying on Egypt for military support runs throughout prophetic literature:

When you have come into the land that the Lord your God is giving you, and you possess it and settle in it and say, "I will set ['asimah] a king over me, like all the nations that are around me," you may indeed set a king over you whom the Lord your God will choose [...] but he must not acquire many horses for himself, or cause the people to return to Egypt in order to acquire horses, for the Lord has said to you, "You shall never return this way again." (Deut 17:14-16)

The warning is echoed by Isaiah:

O, rebellious children, says the Lord,
who take counsel, but not with me;
who devise plans, but not of my spirit,
adding sin to sin;
who set out to go down to Egypt
without asking for my counsel,
to take refuge in the protection of Pharaoh,
and to seek shelter in the shadow of Egypt;
Therefore the strength of Pharaoh shall become your shame,
and trust in the shadow of Egypt your humiliation. (Isa 30:1-3)

And again,

Alas for those who go down to Egypt for help,
who rely on horses,
who trust in chariots because they are many,
and in horsemen because they are very strong,
but do not look to the Holy One of Israel
or seek the Lord! (Isa 31:1)

Despite these warnings, Israel's king Hoshea seeks military support from Egypt in his rebellion against Assyria, which turns out to be a foolhardy move resulting in deportation, destruction, and demise of the northern kingdom:

King Shalmaneser of Assyria came up against Hoshea, who became his vassal ['ebed] and paid him tribute. But the king of Assyria discovered betrayal [qesher] in Hoshea, for he had sent messengers to king So of Egypt and brought no tribute to the king of Assyria as he had done yearly. Therefore, the king of Assyria bound and imprisoned him. Then the king of Assyria invaded all the land and came to Samaria. For three years he besieged it, and in the ninth year of Hoshea the king of Assyria captured Samaria and de the Israelites away to Assyria. (2 Kgs 17:3-6)

Roughly two decades later, king Hezekiah makes overtures toward Egypt in hopes of securing military support against the Assyrians. However, Egypt's reputation as an unreliable ally is known even to Judah's enemies:

> The Rabshakeh said to them, "Say to Hezekiah: Thus says the great king, the king of Assyria [. . .] "In whom do you trust, that you have rebelled against me? See, you trust in the staff of a broken reed [*mish'enet haqqaneh harasus*], this Egypt, which pierces the hand of anyone who leans on it. Such is Pharaoh king of Egypt to all who trust in him. But if you say to me, 'We rely on the Lord our God,' is it not he whose high places and altars Hezekiah has removed, saying to Judah and to Jerusalem, "You shall worship before this altar in Jerusalem"? Now, therefore, I urge you to make a pledge with my master, the king of Assyria, and I will give you 2,000 horses if you are able on your part to set riders on them. How then will you repel the face of one captain, the least of my master's servants, when you put trust in Egypt for chariots and for horsemen? (2 Kgs 18:19-24)

Besides Egypt, other enemies that have extensive military resources include the Canaanite tribes of the conquest narratives. King Jabin of Hazor—a powerful Bronze Age city-state well attested in Egyptian texts and remembered by the Bible writer as the former "head of all these kingdoms" (*rosh kal-hammelakot*)—assembles a large coalition of petty kings to meet the advance of Joshua and the Israelites. This massive assault brought troops "as numerous as the sand along the seashore, with very many horses and chariots" (Jos 11:4), but the battle is one of many in a holy war in which the Divine Warrior fights on behalf of the Israelites, whose obedience allows them to win the day.[9] In another instance, Canaanites dwelling in the Jezreel valley and Beth-She'an are said to have so many iron chariots that the tribes of Joseph (Ephraim and Manasseh), a "numerous

---

[9] See Millard C. Lind, *Yahweh is a Warrior* (Scottdale, PA: Herald Press, 1980).

people" are too afraid to advance against them. Nevertheless, Joshua tells them they shall "drive out the Canaanites, even though they have chariots of iron and are powerful" (Jos 17:14-18). Finally, king Jabin's general, Sisera, commands 900 chariots against Deborah and Barak; nevertheless, the Israelites remain obedient to the Lord so that justice prevails, as Sisera is dispatched by the hand of Yael (Jud 4:12-23).

Reading further along in the Deuteronomistic narratives, we see that no number is given for the number of chariots at David's disposal, yet in the triumphalist early draft of the royal historiography David manages to remain victorious over his enemies' vast military resources. The biblical account of the united monarchy appears to mark an intermediary stage in the later development toward scripture that continues to rely on the exaggeration of enemy resources; here it appears to be for the purpose of glorifying king David, which points to the earlier version of the Deuteronomistic history (Dtr[1]). It recounts David's success in defeating the Philistines, Amelekites, Ammonites, Moabites, and Edomites (2 Samuel 8). Moreover, he strikes down the Aramean King Hadadezer near the Euphrates River, capturing 1,700 charioteers (*parashim*) and 20,000 infantrymen (*ragli*). And when Hadadezer's reinforcements arrive from Damascus, David kills an additional 22,000, drafting the survivors as mercenaries and installing them in new garrisons along Israel's northern border. David then returns to his home in the south, whereupon he kills 14,000 Edomites near the Dead (Salt) Sea.[10] Not long after that, David responds to an affront by the Ammonites, who have secured support from 33,000 Aramean troops (2 Samuel 10). His generals, Joab and Abishai, repel the Arameans and Ammonites respectively, but when the Arameans resolved to array

---

[10] The MT reads Arameans here, but 1 Chr 18:12 and the LXX reads Edomite and Idumean respectively. Add to this the geographical location of the incident, one can only conclude that the MT preserves a scribal error. It should also be noted that the Chronicler ascribes the slaughter to the hand of Abishai, David's military commander and cousin.

themselves against David, he kills 700 chariot teams (*rekeb*) and 40,000 horsemen (*parashim*). By contrast, the Chronicler's account of the battle (1 Chr. 19:18) inflates the number of enemy chariots to 7,000 and replaces horsemen (*parashim*) with infantrymen (*ragli*).

These hyperbolic numbers serve to aggrandize David's royal military prowess, but it seems he manages to accomplish these victories not by having chariots of his own, but with divine assistance. Such material favorable to Israel's early kings must certainly belong to older traditions such as those most likely recorded in the lost *Annals of the Kings of Judah*. Triumphal stories of kingly glory seem to have been retained by later editors (Dtr[2]) to demonstrate just how far human kings can fall: the tall and handsome warrior Saul succumbs to madness and comes to a tragic end, and the final battles of the valiant youthful warrior David come to be waged in his own court (2 Sam. 12:10-11), and so on. Oddly, the earlier, triumphalist version of the Deuteronomistic history (Dtr[1]) accords Solomon a fleet of 1,400 chariots and 40,000 stalls for his horses (1 Kgs 10:26), yet because David spends his reign vanquishing Israel's enemies, Solomon's military goes undeployed. As a result of his idolatry, God splits the kingdom, although not until after his death. In the end, the Bible magnifies the reigns of David and Solomon well beyond the petty chiefdoms that archaeology shows they would have been and retains the material to show how far the kings could fall.

Moving now to the divided monarchy, we see that the number of enemy chariots becomes somewhat more realistic. What persists is the prophetic assertion that Israel's enemies are brought on or restrained only by God's will. The trend continues to be reflected in the story of the first post-Solomonic king, Rehoboam, which foreshadows the eventual destruction of Jerusalem and its temple because of the sins of king and nation, including the account of the looting of the temple by the

Egyptian king Shishak (1 Kgs 14:22-28), an event the Chronicler describes in greater detail:

> And it came to pass that after Rehoboam established his kingdom and he became strong, he and all Israel with him abandoned the law of the Lord. And because they had transgressed against the Lord, in the fifth year of king Rehoboam, king Shishak of Egypt came up against Jerusalem with 1,200 chariots and 60,000 horsemen, and innumerable troops of Libyans, Sukkites and Cushites, which he brought with him from Egypt. He captured the fortified cities of Judah and came as far as Jerusalem. (2 Chr 12:1-4)

This crisis prompts the word of the Lord through the prophet Shemaiah to proclaim, "This is what the Lord says, 'Since you have forsaken me, I now leave you in the hand of Shishak.'" In the face of certain destruction, the king's humility leads to Jerusalem's deliverance, prompting Shemaiah to proclaim Yahweh's mercy in keeping the Egyptian king from attacking Jerusalem, "so that they may learn the difference between serving me and serving kings of the earth." (2 Chr 12:8)[11]

In another account, king Asa's army of 580,000 troops from Judah and Benjamin are attacked by Zerah the Cushite's army of one million men and 300 chariots. Seeing he is outnumbered, Asa cries out:

> O Lord, there is no difference for you between helping the mighty and the weak. Help us, O Lord our God, for we rely on you, and in your name we have come against this multitude. O Lord, you are our God; let no mortal prevail against you.

---

[11] As noted in the previous section, there are problems in attempting to reconcile the biblical Shishak (cf. 1 Kgs. 11:40), with the Shoshenq I of history, who ruled Twenty-second Dynasty Egypt between roughly 943–922 BCE. The historical king's exploits throughout the southern Levant, conducted a few years before his death, are illustrated in the Bubastite Portal reliefs at Karnak and attested in a stela found at Tel Megiddo; however, Jerusalem is not listed among the conquered cities. Conservative viewpoints account for this by suggesting that Rehoboam bought Jerusalem's protection by paying heavy tribute, but it seems unlikely the pharaoh would have exempted the city from his list of regional conquests for that reason.

The victory that follows is not credited to Asa but Yahweh, for as the Chronicler concludes, "So the Lord defeated the Cushites" (2 Chr 14:8-12).

As we saw in Chapter Two, kings of the Bible are cast in an unfavorable light, with kings of the northern kingdom especially criticized. Ahab, for example, is victorious in skirmishes with the more numerous Arameans, but like Saul, he fails to understand that he is not the one in charge, rather it is the Lord (1 Kgs 20:13). In one episode, Ahab confronts Ben-hadad's coalition of thirty-two kings, but the great slaughter (*makkah gedolah*) is attributed to the hand of the Lord (1 Kgs. 20:21). In another instance, the Israelites encamp in two groups in anticipation of yet another Aramean attack. They are described as "two little flocks of goats" (*kishne hasipe 'izzim*), in contrast to vast Aramean forces said to appear as to fill the land (*mil'u 'et-ha'aretz*; 1 Kgs 20:27). Despite the apparent one-sidedness, the Lord leads the Israelites in victory against the coalition's chariots, resulting in the deaths of 100,000 enemy infantrymen (*ragli*) in a single day. The surviving Aramean forces retreat to nearby Aphek, where an additional 27,000 soldiers are crushed under the collapse of the city wall (1 Kgs 20:29-30). In both instances, unnamed prophets advise Ahab of the reason Israel is made to be victorious. It is not Ahab's skills as a warrior king, but the Lord who wins the battles (vv. 13, 28; cf. Exod 14:18). At no point is Ahab credited with victories against these overwhelming enemy forces.

Sometime later, Ahab teams up with king Jehoshaphat of Judah in order to wrest the city of Ramoth-gilead from Aramean control. Before striking out, he consults with his court prophets for a word about the outcome. They tell him, "Go up and succeed [*'elah vehaslah*]; the Lord will give it in the hand of the king" (1 Kgs 22:12). Jehoshaphat then encourages him to make an inquiry of the prophet Micaiah as well, to which Ahab complains that Micaiah never portends anything good for him. Nevertheless, he inquires of Micaiah, who also tells him the same thing, "Go up and succeed; the Lord will give it into the hand of the king" (v. 15). In both cases, the root of the verb "succeed," *salah* is in the verbal form (*hiphil*) used to signify causation in the active voice. There is nothing wrong with the translation as it stands, but it presents an ambiguity that could apply to either king. So, it is not exactly a lying breath that comes from the prophets, just a misleading one.

When Ahab presses Micaiah further, the prophet utters a word from the Lord that Ahab does not want to hear, namely that Israel's king would be struck down and his soldiers scattered. When Ahab angrily demands an explanation, Micaiah informs him that the positive outcome predicted by his court prophets was the result of a lying breath (*ruach sheqer*) the Lord had placed in their mouths, so that Ahab might die in the battle for Ramoth-gilead (1 Kgs 22:19-23). Still, Ahab disguises himself to hide his kingly status, leaving Jehoshaphat as the only one arrayed in royal garb, and sets out in battle against the king of Aram and his thirty-two chariot captains (*sare harekeb*). Despite his nondescript disguise, a fateful arrow strikes Ahab. By evening he dies, and as predicted (1 Kgs 21:19), dogs lick up his blood (1 Kgs 22:38).

To be sure, the biblical scribe has written at great length about king Ahab—hundreds of lines recounting all his poor decisions and idolatrous actions, all of which lead him deeply into the Lord's disfavor toward a violent and ignominious death. However, the pathetic king Ahab of the Bible looks nothing like the valiant Ahab of history known from the Assyrian, Aramean, and Moabite inscriptions described above. Instead, the writer sets down only what he wants his readers to know:

> Now the rest of the acts of Ahab, and all that he did, and the ivory house that he built, and all the cities that he built, are they not written in the Book of the Annals of the Kings of Israel? (1 Kgs 22:39)

The literary strategy should now be very clear in the prophetic affirmation that the Lord is commander-in-chief of the inhabited world, with power that extends well beyond Israel. The Lord leads Babylon's chariots to blaze like lightning through the streets of Nineveh (Nah 2:3-4, 13), brings Pharaoh's chariots against Philistia (Jer 47:1-4), and pits the Medes and Persians against Babylon (Jer 51:1-2, 11). For Israel, the tide of battle rises and falls on obedience to Yahweh's command, which proves to be a losing proposition for God's people from the start of the Deuteronomistic history (Former Prophets) to the end. The story of entrance into the Promised Land in Joshua ends with Israel's expulsion from it in 2 Kings.

The role of the fiery chariots and horses is rooted in God's readiness to fight on behalf of Israel before they enter the Promised Land (Exod 14:13-14; Deut 7:17-19; 20:1). This conviction continues into the historiographical narratives as well, for as the Chronicler asserts, the Lord will fight back Judah's restless neighbors:

> Thus says the Lord to you: "Do not fear or be dismayed at this great multitude; for the battle is not yours but God's. ... This battle is not for you to fight; take your position, stand still, and see the victory of the Lord on your behalf, O Judah and Jerusalem." (2 Chr. 20:15)

God's military resources are also extolled in the Psalms, where chariots of iron are outnumbered by chariots of the divine— "mighty chariots, twice ten thousand, thousands upon thousands" (Ps 68:17), which remain Israel's true hope:

> Some trust in chariots and some in horses, but we trust in the name of the Lord our God (Ps 20:7)

> With the Lord on my side, I do not fear. What can mortals do to me?" (Ps 118:6)

In 2 Kings 2, Yahweh's forces are imaged as chariots and horses of fire (*rekeb 'esh ve-sus 'esh*). Following Elijah's outrageous demonstration of power on Mt. Carmel, in which he puts Jezebel's 450 prophets of Baal to shame and slaughters them in a ravine (1 Kgs 18:20-40), the prophet flees southward all the way to Beer-sheba. From there he is instructed by the Lord's messenger to go into the wilderness (*midbar*) and then to Horeb, the mountain of God, where at the end of his useful life he receives his greatest tasks. He is ordered to execute coups d'etat in Damascus and Samaria, after which he may appoint a successor (1 Kgs 19:15-18). Fortunately for him, the worn-out prophet first encounters Elisha, who sticks with his master like a shadow wherever he is sent (2 Kgs 2:1-8)

No motive is given for Yahweh's arbitrary command to move Elijah from Gilgal to Bethel and back to Jericho, near the place he began, but that's precisely the point. Prophets are instruments of the Lord. As with Elijah, Yahweh drives the prophets and drives them further until they are ready to drop, even to the point where they may be ready to yield up their lives; but it is the Lord who decides when they are done. Deut 34:7 states that Moses was 120 years old, yet "his eyes were undimmed and his vigor unabated," basically meaning he needed neither glasses nor sexual enhancements. Why mention these youthful qualities at all except to make the point that God decides when he is finished with the prophet.

A question arises over which Gilgal the master and disciple were sent from, for there are at least a few places with that name. The first place that comes to mind is the spot on the western bank of the Jordan, near Jericho. There the Israelites made their camp after crossing over from Moab, setting up stones representing each of the twelve tribes. Indeed, *gilgal* refers to a circle of upright stones, a phenomenon found in other places throughout the region. The Bible mentions a Gilgal in the mountains of Samaria near Shechem (Deut 11:29-30; cf. Gen 12:6), and another on the border between Judah and Benjamin, not far from Bethel. It is the latter Gilgal that most scholars believe the biblical writer had in mind since the text says they "went down to Bethel (v. 2), arguing that the one farther north, or the one near Jericho would each be too far away. But that's the point: God is not required to be reasonable.

The distance from Gilgal (the one nearer to Jericho) to Bethel is roughly fifteen miles as the crow flies, but Elijah and his disciple are not birds. They must walk a winding path that climbs at a very steep grade—from some 800 feet below sea level, to more than 2800 feet above sea level. The text says they went down (*yarad*) to Bethel, but that does not mean they went south, for the directions we are accustomed to do not obtain in the ancient world. Going up did not mean going north; it meant going uphill. Once Elijah and Elijah make it to the highest ridge, they would descend to the shallow valley in which Bethel is nestled.

Once in Bethel, the site of a centuries-old Levitical shrine re-purposed by king Jeroboam I in 1 Kings 12, Elisha is beset by annoying sons of the prophets, who swarm like mosquitoes around his ears telling him something he already knows: "Do you know that today the Lord will take your master away from you?" To which he replies something to the effect of, "Yes, I know. Shut up!" Immediately, Elijah is commanded to go to Jericho, essentially returning to the place they began. The absurdity of the itinerary demonstrates Elisha's loyalty and suitability for succeeding his master, for who else would engage in such slavish, seemingly pointless obedience? In all of this Elisha proves himself a worthy recipient of the difficult thing (*qashah*) he is about to receive:

> And it came to pass that when they had crossed over, Elijah said to Elisha, "Tell me what I may do for you, before I am taken from you." Elisha said, "Please let there be a double portion of your spirit upon me [*pi-shenayîm beruhaka 'elay*]." He responded, "You have asked a difficult thing. Nevertheless, if you see me as I am being taken from you, it will be granted you; if not, it will not." As they continued walking and talking, a chariot [or chariots] of fire and horses of fire separated the two of them, and Elijah ascended in a whirlwind [*basse'arah*] into heaven. Elisha kept watching and crying out, "My father! My father! The chariots of Israel and its horsemen!" But when he could no longer see him,

he grasped his own clothes and tore them in two pieces.
(vv. 9-12)

Elisha's request for a double portion of his master's spirit does
not mean he is asking to be twice the prophet Elijah has
become; rather, he is asking to become the master's *bekor*, or
firstborn son—a special category that entitles the eldest son to
inherit the greater share (two-thirds) of his father's estate. Of
course, this point has nothing to do with the inherited portion,
especially since there are no other sons in contention, but
everything to do with the fact that what we have here is a
succession narrative. If Elisha sees his master as he is being
taken up from him, his request—which Elijah rightly calls a
difficult thing—will be granted. It is also incumbent upon the
reader/hearer to "see."

Because *rekeb* can serve as a collective noun, the distinction
between singular and plural is not all that clear and is usually
determined on the basis of context. In many cases, it would be
better to translate *rekeb* as chariotry. Most translations posit that
a single chariot passes between them, but there is sufficient
reason to imagine the writer had in mind a column of fiery
chariots. Whichever the case, it is telling that the verb usually
translated "divide" or "separated" (*hibdil*) is not used here, but
yaprid, which can mean something passing between them that
connects them, forming a kind of link—prophetic succession, if
you will. Thus, with respect to the hymnodic and iconographic
traditions, as well as theological commentary commending
Elijah into the heavens in a fiery chariot, such an image is not
supported by the text. At any rate, the reader /hearer "sees"
what was is meant to be seen, namely, the Lord's own chariotry
bridging the strange pair. But what might all this mean?

As we saw in the first section above, teams of iron chariots
were an ancient kingdom's highest and best line of defense;
however, as shown in the second section, the biblical writer has
other ideas about such technology. With the advantage of
20-20 hindsight, it was clear that chariots of iron did not provide

the protection they promised; thus, Judah's trust was entirely misspent. It should have been invested in the Word of God all along—well before it was too late, beyond any hope for deliverance.

The imagery of fire chariots continues in 2 Kgs 6:8-23, where the king of Aram (Syria) is said to be launching repeated raids against Israel's towns and villages, only to be intercepted by the Israelite army mobilized in anticipation of his every move. Frustrated by his inability to take these cities by surprise, the Aramean king begins to suspect he has a spy among his ranks. When one of his advisers informs him that he is being thwarted by Elisha, who knows every word the king speaks, even in the privacy of his own bedchamber (v. 12), the king redirects his forces toward finding Elisha. When the king learns the prophet has been spotted in Dothan he sends "horses and chariots and a great army" by night to surround the city (v. 14). Early next morning, Elisha's servant steps outside and sees the vast enemy army. Trembling with fear, he implores Elisha to tell him what to do, to which the prophet calmly replies, "Do not be afraid, for we outnumber them." Elisha then prays that the eyes of the servant be opened:

> So the LORD opened the eyes of the servant, and he saw; the mountain was full of horses and chariots of fire all round Elisha. (v. 17)

As the Arameans begin to attack, Elisha prays to the Lord that they all be struck blind. He then rounds up the helpless warriors and delivers them to the king of Israel, who acknowledges Elisha's power and authority by addressing him as "my father" (*'abi*) and then defers to his advice (vv. 21-22). Elisha allows the Aramean charioteers and foot soldiers to return to their country as a witness to the power of Israel's God.

The fiery chariot motif appears yet again in 2 Kgs 13:14, where the king utters the exact words Elisha had spoken as his master ascended into the heavens in a whirlwind:

Now when Elisha had fallen sick with the illness of which he was to die, Joash king of Israel went down to him, and wept before him, crying, "My father, my father! The chariots of Israel and its horsemen!"

The repetition of these words in these new contexts—spoken by no less than kings—indicates that the image of fiery chariots and horses is being used as a literary motif that symbolizes divine power at work through the spiritual lineage of the true biblical prophets. What originally circulated as separate legends about two charismatic prophetic figures have been brought together in a succession narrative emphasizing the transfer of prophetic power and authority through a particular prophetic lineage, an assertion supported by the fact that the two *coups d'état* assigned to Elijah in 1 Kgs 18:15-16 are carried out *by God through Elisha* in 2 Kgs 9:1-11 and 10:1-11 respectively.

In sum, the prophetic perspective asserts that Israel's and Judah's chariots of iron are yet another human-made repository for misplaced trust, and that these kingdoms' highest and best line of defense is to be found in the Word of God passed along through the line of true biblical prophets. The line extends through the entirety of the biblical story from Moses, through Elijah and Elisha, and on to his "prophet like me" (Deut 18:15), a seventh-century BCE prophet from the Deuteronomist writer's own time, almost certainly Jeremiah.[12] The point here is that Israel's and Judah's lack of obedience and failure to trust in Yahweh's fiery chariots and horses brought these forces against them.

Conclusion

We have seen the wide chasm that exists between the real world of Iron Age chariots and the timeless prophetic

---

[12] Isaac Abravanel (Abarbanel), a 15th C Portuguese Jewish sage, seems to be the first scholar on record to have expressed this view. If R. Friedman is correct in suggesting that the author is Jeremiah's scribe, Baruch ben Neriah, then the identification becomes even more likely. See Richard E. Friedman, *Who Wrote the Bible?* (San Francisco: Harper Collins Publishers, 1997), 147-48.

perspective, which asserts the God of Scripture wields the world's weapons of war with his outstretched hand, a display of might that demonstrates unsurpassed glory and might (Exod 14:15, 18). The prophets make it clear that obedience to God's will in maintaining justice and righteousness throughout the world protects a nation from his terrible wrath. For Israel, this would have meant reaping the benefits of peace, prosperity, and protection from its divine Shepherd, but its disobedience to the Yahweh and his statutes brought it face to face with its Warrior God.

The prophetic warning that God would turn against his own people is not entirely unique. As mentioned in the previous chapter, the best known example is the late-third millennium BCE epic of the fall of Akkad, in which the storm deity Enlil brings the Gutians against the city for the sins of king Naram-Sin, compelling Inanna/Ishtar to abandon her own temple and join the assault. Furthermore, the aforementioned Moabite inscription implies that the House of Omri was able to conquer neighboring Moab because of Chemosh's displeasure over the Moabites' lack of due worship. Similarly, God employs the armies of Assyria and Babylon against Samaria and Jerusalem respectively, the former due to the persistent "sins of Jeroboam" (2 Kgs 17:21-23), and the latter because of the sins of Manasseh:

> Nevertheless, the Lord did not turn from the fierceness of his great wrath by which his anger was stirred up against Judah, because of all the provocations with which Manasseh had provoked him. The Lord said, "I will remove Judah also out of my sight, as I have removed Israel; and I will cast off this city that I have chosen, and Jerusalem, and the house of which I said, My name shall be there." (2 Kgs 23:26-27)

Ironically, an obvious interpolation in the book of Hosea inserted at some point during the roughly 135-year period between the destructions of Samaria and Jerusalem, asserts that earthly defenses are of no avail for a disobedient nation that trusts in its own power:

But I [the Lord] will have pity on the house of Judah, and I will save them by the Lord their God; I will not save them by bow, or by sword, or by war, or by horses, or by horsemen." (Hos 1:7)

Although Priestly texts assert that Israel is made holy through obedience (e.g., Lev. 20:24; cf. 11:44; 19:2; 20:25-26; 22:32), both the Former and Latter prophets assert that Israel is unable to attain holiness because of its inability to attain justice and righteousness.[13] In the book of Hosea, God abandons Israel completely.

When she had weaned Lo-ruhamah, she conceived and bore a son. Then the Lord said, "Name him Lo-ammi, for you are no longer my people and I am no longer your God." (Hos 1:8-9)

According to the word of the Lord through Hosea, Israel's idolatry will not go unpunished:

. . . and she [Gomer] conceived and bore him a son. And the Lord said to him, "Name him Jezreel, for in a little while I will punish the house of Jehu for the blood of Jezreel, and I will put an end to the kingdom of the house of Israel. On that day I will break the bow of Israel in the valley of Jezreel."

For the priestly scribes who heeded the prophets, the cause of the destruction of Jerusalem, and Samaria was clear. The Lord had directed swarms of enemy chariots, along with other sorts of calamities—famine, pestilence, etc.—against these disobedient cities. Hindsight was 20/20, witnessing to the fact that Israel's iron chariots were unable to deliver Jerusalem from the hand of the living God. Such misplaced trust in works of the

---

[13] Deuteronomic jurisprudence contrasts sharply with the Priestly codes. Generally speaking, the centrality of priestly ritual holiness is of lesser importance to Deuteronomic advocates of a social and religious order based primarily on prophetic justice (see Deut 21:1-9). The Priestly writings view holiness as something dynamic, dangerous, and having a power all its own, thus requiring highly specialized technicians and restricted access. By contrast, the Deuteronomist views holiness as less a dangerous power than a status one acquires through the dedicated application of wisdom, morality, and justice. See Philip P. Jenson, *Graded Holiness: A Key to the Priestly Conception of the World*. JSOTSup 106. Sheffield: Sheffield Academic Press, 1992; and Eyal Regev, "Priestly Dynamic Holiness and Deuteronomic Static Holiness." *VT* 51, no. 2 (2001): 243-261.

hands is tantamount to idolatry, a perspective that would contribute to the eventual rise of scripture, for as Tarazi asserts,

> The scriptural story [. . .] depicts the sad story of the scriptural Israel while blaming it not on the aggressor's overwhelming power, but rather on Israel's recalcitrant disobedience to the scriptural God generation after generation.[14]

The prophetic critique of over-reliance on military weaponry, as exemplified by extravagant budgets leading to burgeoning arsenals in the US, is as relevant as ever, especially given that current nuclear stockpiles have the potential to destroy the world many times over. After all, it only takes once. Raising loud voices against bloated spending and burgeoning reserves would seem to be the prophetic thing to do. It takes faith and courage to counter the narrative of politicians and the lobbyists who buy them, which appeals to the fears and insecurities of an uninformed citizenry, but true wisdom leaves outcomes to God. The reader should understand that the Bible does not discourage taking reasonable defensive measures, but it does warn against a nation investing trust in works of the hands at a level tantamount to idolatry, leading an arrogant nation to believe its security can be guaranteed by means of its own technology of death and destruction:

> But if you hearken carefully to me, says the Lord, to bring no burden through the gates of this city on the sabbath day, but devote the sabbath day holy to do no work on it, then there shall enter by the gates of this city kings and princes sitting on the throne of David, riding in chariots and on horses, they and their officials, the men of Judah and the inhabitants of Jerusalem; and this city shall be inhabited forever. (Jer 17:24-25; cf. 22:4)

A pipe dream, to be sure.

---

[14] Paul Nadim Tarazi, *Decoding Genesis 1–11* (St. Paul, MN: OCABS Press, 2020), 106.

Chapter 5
The Trouble with Political Economy

Do not say to yourself, "My power and the might of my own hand have gotten me this wealth." But remember the Lord your God, for it is he who gives you power to get wealth. (Deut 8:17-18a)

For wicked men are found among my people; they ensnare men like fowlers waiting to trap birds. (Jer 5:26)

On July 13, 2012, former US President Barack Obama delivered a re-election campaign speech in Roanoke, VA, during which the refrain, "You didn't build that!" highlighted governmental support in cultivating economic growth in the private sector. The phrase was immediately seized upon by the conservative blogosphere, which removed it from context and reframed it as an insult to business owners who should be taking sole credit for their entrepreneurial successes. Of course, the world of business is not so simple, as success depends on the ability to secure ready capital or navigate existing laws and tax benefits in an economic system arguably fixed by those who stand to benefit most from it. In the end, economics in the US and around the world cannot be fully understood apart from politics and vice versa. Reapplying James Carville's well-known quip from Bill Clinton's 1992 presidential campaign, "It's the economy stupid."

Of course, there is great disparity between political and economic systems past and present. However, the phrase "You didn't build that" can be applied in any age of history, and effectively sums up Moses's solemn warning at the threshold of the Promised Land:

Take care that you do not forget the Lord your God by failing to keep his commandments, his ordinances, and his statutes that I am commanding you today. When you have eaten your fill and have built fine houses and live in them and when your herds and flocks have multiplied and your silver and gold is multiplied and all that you have is multiplied, then do not exalt yourself, forgetting the Lord your God who brought you out of the land of Egypt [. . .]. Do not say to yourself, "My power and the might of my own hand have gotten me this wealth." But remember the Lord your God, for it is he who gives you power to get wealth, so that he may confirm his covenant that he swore to your ancestors, as he is doing today. If you do forget the Lord your God and follow other gods to serve and worship them, I solemnly warn you today that you shall surely perish. Like the nations that the Lord is destroying before you, so shall you perish, because you would not obey the voice of the Lord your God. (Deut 8:11-20)

Moses's admonition to remember the Lord as the source of all earthly beneficence is framed by stern warnings of obedience to the demands of the Torah on the one hand, and a consequential prophecy *ex eventu* on the other hand. This chapter compares the prophetic critique of Israel's political economy within the context of the ancient Near East in a way that informs thinking scripturally about political and economic justice today.

Political Economy in the Ancient Near East[1]

The earliest settlements in ancient Mesopotamia were kin-based, cooperative, and relatively egalitarian. Settlers lived in tents or other simple structures made of reeds and mudbrick, making it easy to relocate in times of flood or famine or resume pastoral migration with long-term changes in climate. The details of everyday life are all but lost to history, but archaeology and reasoned imagination help create a reliable general picture. Material remains of modest domiciles suggest that the nuclear family was the basic social unit, consisting of a man and woman and their children along with perhaps one or more elderly parents. Over time, additional rooms were added to accommodate growth, or another house was constructed that

---

[1] Simply stated, political economy is a sociological concept used in analyzing the relationship between a society's sociopolitical organization and its acquisition, management, and distribution of resources.

shared an adjoining wall. Days were spent planting, tending, or harvesting grain and vegetables; gathering wild foodstuffs; grinding grains for bread and preparing stews; and raising sheep and goats.

As one would expect of a labor-intensive agricultural society, economic needs were met cooperatively. Able-bodied family members, both male and female, worked the fields at all hours of the day and tended to the animals. A burial report from Late Bronze Age tombs at Tel Gezer is especially telling. It reveals that the average life span for its inhabitants "did not exceed thirty years of age," and that the most of the bodies examined, both male and female, revealed suffering from severe osteoarthritis in the lumbar vertebrae from spending so much of their life in a stooped-over position—plowing, sowing, hoeing, and reaping in the fields.[2] In addition to this, women undertook perilous duties in bearing and raising the children needed for sustaining and replenishing the labor force. At any rate, largely egalitarian cooperation and shared distribution of resources meant feast or famine for all members of the settlement. It is interesting to think that with the absence of a centralized, exploitative elite there can be no concept of "the poor."

With the rise of more complex societies and city states, regional resources of grain, animals, and manpower once shared among the inhabitants of rural settlements falls at least in part under the control of the king and members of the ruling elite. The real-life cost of maintaining a centralized authority is reflected in Samuel's warning to Israel concerning the ways of a king (1 Sam 8:11-18).

> This will be the way of the king that shall reign over you: he will take your sons and appoint them to his chariots and to be his horsemen, and they shall run before his chariots, and he will appoint them for himself as commanders of thousands and

---

[2] *Gezer V: The Field I Caves*, eds. Joe D. Seger and H. Darrell Lance (Jerusalem: Hebrew Union College/Nelson Gleuck School of Biblical Archaeology, 1988) 130-31.

commanders of fifties; and some to plow his ground and reap his harvest, and to make his implements of war and the equipment of his chariots. And he will take your daughters to be perfumers and cooks and bakers. And he will take the best of your fields and vineyards and olive orchards and give them to his servants. He will take one-tenth of your grain and of your vineyards and give it to his officers and his courtiers. He will take your male and female slaves and the best of your cattle and donkeys and put them to his work. He will take one-tenth of your flocks, and you shall be his slaves. And on that day you will cry out because of your king, whom you have chosen for yourselves, but the Lord will not answer you on that day. (1 Sam 8:1-11).

The Hebrew text of this passage does not actually repeat the verb "to take" (*laqach*) as often as it appears in translation, but the staccato repetition of the *ve-eth* construction that precedes each object in the litany of things the king will snatch from his subjects is effective in making the point that an anguished people will eventually cry out because of the excessive material demands of their kings, who have no qualms about satisfying their own needs and desires at the expense of their subjects. Samuel warns the elders that although they may cry out, "the Lord will not answer you on that day." The fact that the earthly king takes what he wants for no other reason than because he can, is whimsically portrayed in comedian Mel Brooks's character Louis XIV in *History of the World, Part I* (1981), who proclaims, "It's good to be the king!" However, earthly kings contrast sharply with the scripture's heavenly King, who demands strict obedience but rewards abundantly. In recounting the demands of the king, the biblical account reflects the greater social stratification and expanding networks of power common to Iron Age kingdoms west of the Euphrates. The resulting disparity and social injustice is decried by the prophets, most notably Amos and Hosea.

The Prophetic Critique of Israel's Political Economy

The best biblical example of extreme socioeconomic injustice committed by a leader in a position of power over an innocent person is the poignant account of Ahab over Naboth (1 Kings 21). The story takes place in the fertile Jezreel valley, where Naboth's ancestral estate bordered Ahab and Jezebel's palace. Naboth's land was a vast vineyard, but the king desired it for purposes of turning it into a vegetable garden (*gan yaraq*), presumably for his own private use. Ahab's desire to cultivate herbs and vegetables as a replacement for an established vineyard seems odd considering the significant economic value of wine production for the kingdom, a thriving industry supported by recent excavations at Tel Jezreel. Ahab asks Naboth to give him the land in exchange for a plot of comparable worth elsewhere or the equivalent of its worth in silver. However, according to the law, Naboth's land could not actually be sold for it belongs to Yahweh: "And the land shall not be sold in perpetuity, for the land is mine; to me you are but aliens and tenants" (Lev 25:23).[3] Thus, Naboth refuses, saying "God forbid that I should give the inheritance of my fathers to you!" (v. 3).

At first, the king acquiesces, although it is not clear whether he is compelled by actual law or established custom. Either way, the disappointment of not getting what he wants festers into full-blown obsession. The description of the king's visceral agony— to the point of withdrawing to his couch and refusing to eat— seems greatly overplayed, but it sets up the scheme of his Phoenician queen Jezebel, who urges her husband to exploit his royal power and seize the land for himself. She sends out letters

---

[3] Biblical laws are inconsistent when it comes to property rights over time, but they all agree that land is a family's most valuable economic asset. In times of financial distress, all or parts of a family's rights to an inherited estate could be sold to an outside buyer; however, as the story of Ruth illustrates (ch. 4) the right to redeem it was an expected legal right.

in the king's name calling for a public fast (*tsom*) at which Naboth would be seated at the head of the assembly, then secretly arranges for two witnesses to falsely charge him with cursing God and king. Facing the false public charge of treason, Naboth is escorted out of the city and unjustly executed (v. 13), leaving Ahab free to confiscate Naboth's estate. Unlike the real world, justice ultimately prevails in the narrative world over which the God of Scripture rules; so although the wicked couple initially succeeds in executing their nefarious plan, the Lord's hitman, the prophet Elijah the Tishbite, publicly extols their impending demise at the mouths of ravenous dogs (vv. 17-23). Unfortunately, real-world stewards of a nation's political economy cannot always be trusted to safeguard justice, but in scripture, God always has the final word.

Tragic stories such as Naboth's find reflection in the words of earlier, eighth century BCE prophets like Amos and Hosea, whose scathing critiques of the socioeconomic status quo rooted in the Mosaic standard of justice accurately foretold the utter destruction of the nation. Amos, a shepherd of Tekoa, rails against an economy regulated by the king and sanctioned by his priesthood that allows a certain segment of society to gain wealth by crushing the needy and trampling the poor underfoot.

> Thus says the Lord: For three transgressions of Israel
> and for four, I will not revoke the punishment,
> for they sell the righteous for silver
> and the needy for a pair of sandals—
> they who breathe after dust on the head of the poor
> and shove the humble out of the way;
> father and son go to the same girl
> to profane my holy name,
> and they lay themselves down beside every altar
> upon clothing taken as collateral;
> and in the house of their God they drink
> the wine of those who have been fined. (Amos 2:6-8)

Notice how Amos's oracle condemning Israel's unjust treatment of the poor overshadows the passing mention of father's and son's participation in Canaanite ritual, which given the pervasive symbolism of the bull throughout the north, may be reflected in 4:1-5 as well:

> Hear this word, you cows of Bashan
> who are on Mount Samaria,
> who oppress the poor, who crush the needy,
> who say to their husbands, "Bring something to drink!"
> The Lord God has sworn by his holiness:
> The time is surely coming upon you
> when they shall drag you away with hooks,
> even the last of you with fishhooks.
> Through breaches in the wall you shall leave,
> each one straight ahead,
> and you shall be flung out into Harmon,
> says the Lord. (4:1-3)

At this point, the Lord speaks through Amos in words dripping with scorn:

> Come to Bethel and transgress,
> to Gilgal and multiply transgression!
> Bring your sacrifices in the morning,
> and your tithes every three days;
> and offer a thanksgiving offering of leavened bread
> and proclaim freewill offerings and publish them,
> for so you love to do, O children of Israel! (4:3-5)

As with Naboth, abuses of power will be visited, and justice will prevail:

> Therefore, because you trample upon the poor
> and take from him taxes of grain,
> you have built houses of hewn stone.
> But you shall not live in them.
> You have planted pleasant vineyards,
> but you shall not drink their wine.
> For I know how many are your transgressions
> and how great are your sins,
> you who afflict the righteous, who take a bribe
> and turn aside the needy at the gate. (5:11-13)

As a true biblical prophet who denies being a professional prophet (7:14)—and whose own life as a herdsman and dresser of fig trees may have been impacted by the socioeconomic injustice he rails against—Amos is able to read the signs of his time in ways others cannot. The Day of the Lord, formerly a time of victory and visitation, becomes a day to be feared:

> Woe to you who desire the day of the Lord!
> Why do you want the day of the Lord?
> It is darkness, not light,
> as if someone fled from a lion
> and was met by a bear
> or went into the house and rested a hand against the wall
> and was bitten by a snake.
> Is not the day of the Lord darkness, not light,
> and gloom with no brightness in it? (5:18-20)

These powerful words survive the catastrophe they portended. Assyrian kings Tiglath-Pileser III, Sargon II, and Shalmaneser V soon hammered the northern kingdom of Israel in succession, bringing the nation to the end of its history.

The prophet Hosea, Amos's somewhat later contemporary, also holds Israel's leadership to account for the transgressions of the kingdom and agrees that such a nation cannot endure:[4]

> Hear this, O priests!
> Give heed, O House of Israel!
> Listen, O House of the King!
> For the judgment pertains to you! (Hos 5:1)

The prophet's acerbic taunt recalls Israel's appeal for a in 1 Samuel 8:

> I will destroy you, O Israel;
> who can help you?
> Where now is your king, that he may save you?
> Where in all your cities are your rulers,
> of whom you said,
> "Give me a king and rulers?"

---

[4] See Richard Benton, *Hosea* (St. Paul, MN: OCABS Press, 2021).

I gave you a king in my anger,
and I took him away in my wrath. (Hos 13:9-11)

The books of Amos and Hosea, integrated as they are with the Deuteronomistic worldview for which justice is foundational, serve as compelling precedents for later Judahite prophets like Ezekiel and Jeremiah in proclaiming leadership as being especially vulnerable to the consequences of divine judgment. Although representing conflicting priesthoods and different social backgrounds, Jeremiah and Ezekiel stand united in their condemnation of unjust economic structures sustained by the monarchy that invite destruction upon the nation. The deported Aaronid-Zadokite priest Ezekiel is detached from the temple and altar that occupy the very center of his existence; Jeremiah, son of a Levitical priest from Anatoth, is a despised pariah persecuted for proclaiming Judah's demise. These prophets interpret the impending calamity from different vantage points—each in the language of his own professional experience—yet both assert the inevitability of Jerusalem's destruction. It is not by chance that the books attributed to Ezekiel and Jeremiah, representing two distinct priestly lineages, stand linked together like a unifying diptych at the heart of the Hebrew Bible.

Like Amos, Jeremiah's response to the question of what went wrong is rooted at least in part in the actions of those who prey on the poor and disadvantaged:

For wicked men are found among my people;
like fowlers they lie in wait;
they set a trap that catches men.
Like a cage full of birds,
their houses are full of deceit;
Therefore they have become great and rich,
they have grown fat and sleek.
They know no limit in wicked deeds,
they do not judge with justice
To make prosper the cause of the orphan,
and they do not defend the rights of the needy.

Shall I not punish them for these things, says the Lord,
And shall I not bring retribution
upon a nation such as this? (Jer 5:26-29)

Like the northern prophets before him, Jeremiah reads the signs
of his times bringing imminent judgment upon the nation for
the wicked abuse of power among its royal and priestly leaders.
The fall of the kingdom demonstrates how socioeconomic
injustice results in irrevocable consequences. Likewise, Judah is
brought to the end of its national history as well.

Jeremiah's exiled Aaronid priestly contemporary, Ezekiel,
also chides a system seriously corrupted by the lack of justice
and righteousness among the wealthy and powerful in
neglecting the plight of the orphans and the widows (Ezek 22.7).
The system permits the wealthy to continue the practice of
usury (*neshek*), take unjust gain (*betsa*), and oppress their
neighbors out of lust for their possessions. The prophetic word
accuses them of acquiring the best of everything for themselves
without restoring or replenishing the assets of those from whose
lives they diminish (Ezek 34:3-4). According to Ezekiel's scribes,
these wealthy princes and nobles will be scattered among the
nations like those of the northern kingdom and all their wealth
will melt away as dross (22:18-20).

All true prophets assert that national collapse is divinely
ordered, but Ezekiel provides a reason. A formula reiterated
nearly sixty times throughout the book, Ezekiel proclaims God's
actions are meted out so that "you know that I am the Lord."
Asserting that every person will be responsible for his or her own
deeds and that only the soul that commits the iniquities shall die
(18.3-4), Ezekiel insists that one's personal responsibilities
include extending economic justice to one's fellows. Note that
the failure to do so, as suggested earlier, is tied to idolatry and
that right worship is integrated with right social and political
economy:

If a man be just and perform that which is just and right and does
not eat upon the hills nor lifts his eyes to the idols of the house of

Israel [...] and wrongs no one, but restores collateral for a debt, does not rob, but gives bread to the hungry and clothes the naked; does not lend money with interest, nor take any increase, who withdraws his hand from iniquity and executes true justice between persons, who walks in my statutes and keeps my ordinances to deal truly and is just, *he* shall surely live, says the Lord. (Ezek 18:15-17)

The writer is certainly not unrealistic. He must have known full well that the righteous and just suffer untimely deaths as much as the wicked. But the prophetic world he envisioned equates a life of justice and righteousness (*mishpat ve-tzedakah*) with having achieved a state of ultimate human existence. Indeed, these twinned concepts, to be maintained in balance, provide the basis for a healthy and sustainable political economy.

Justice and Righteousness in Political Economy

Justice (*mishpat*) is a fundamental element of the prophetic perspective that is rooted in the fabric of creation itself. This term, which can also be translated "right judgment," carries the expectation that human relationships should align with divine standards, but as Ezekiel laments, God's ways go unrecognized (Ezek 18:25, 29).

Righteousness (*tzedakah*) is also a concrete term. Like *mishpat*, *tzedakah* is rooted in the principle of equality, a universal concept that all human beings have an innate ability to recognize.[5] When the words *mishpat* and *tzedakah* are paired, as they so often are, they form a *hendiadys*, a synonymous parallelism that opens up a semantic range beyond anything the terms convey independently. The pairing of *mishpat ve-tzedakah* is among the most significant and oft-used attributes of God, found throughout the Prophets and the Psalms. As Lord and King of all creation, the biblical God is the supreme Judge of the world,

---

[5] Given Fr. Paul Tarazi's antipathy towards all things platonic, dare I mention that Plato observes this principle in the *Phaedo* (74a–75a)?

establishing its very foundation and bringing it to fruition in justice and righteousness among all the peoples:

> The Lord is king; let the peoples tremble.
> He sits enthroned upon the cherubim; let the earth quake.
> The Lord is great in Zion;
> he is exalted over all the peoples.
> Let them praise your great and awesome name.
> Holy is he.
> Mighty king, lover of justice,
> you have established equity;
> You have executed justice
> and righteousness in Jacob.
> Extol the Lord our God;
> worship at his footstool.
> Holy is he!

Similarly, Psalm 97 ties justice and righteousness closely with God's sovereign majesty (vv. 1-2):

> The Lord is king! Let the earth rejoice;
> let the many coastal plains be glad.
> Clouds and thick darkness are all around him;
> righteousness and justice are the foundation of his throne.

According to Jeremiah, these divine attributes are to exist together and practiced by those who enjoy power and authority over others:

> Thus says the Lord: Do not let the wise boast in their wisdom, do not let the mighty boast in their might, do not let the wealthy boast in their wealth; but let those who boast boast in this, that they understand and know me, that I am the Lord; I act with steadfast love [*hesed*], justice, and righteousness in the earth; for in these things I delight, says the Lord. (Jer 9:23-24)

The fact that God has established justice in the universe and judges with righteousness from his throne makes it incumbent upon that kings and judges of the earth to do likewise:

> Give the king your justice, O God,
> and your righteousness to a king's son.

May he judge your people with righteousness,
and your poor with justice. (Ps 72:1-2)

The obligation for the royal house to administer justice and righteousness is expected to filter down into other levels of society, the same way that their lack of justice and righteousness filtered down resulting in the destruction of Jerusalem. And so it is that the combination of justice and righteousness, held together in balance, is something expected of all persons in positions of responsibility. As Moberly observes, instances of the pairing *mishpat ve-tzedakah* "consistently refer to those qualities which God seeks in humanity in general and in Israel in particular."[6] To be sure, these terms require pairing on the human plane and must mutually co-arise for righteousness without justice (i.e., "right judgment") can perilously overstep into self-righteousness (e.g., Job and Jonah), while justice without righteousness carries the potential for lacking mercy.

Finally, although not exhaustively, there is the proverb, "To do righteousness and justice is more acceptable to the Lord than sacrifice" (Prov 21:3), no better illustrated than in this oft-quoted passage in Amos, which voices God's disdain for the empty offerings of animal and song in a land where justice and righteousness are lacking:

I hate, I despise your festivals,
and I take no delight in your solemn assemblies.
Even though you offer me your burnt offerings and grain offerings,
I will not accept them,
And the offerings of well-being of your fatted animals
I will not look upon.

Take away from me the noise of your songs;
I will not listen to the melody of your harps.
But let justice roll down like waters,

---

[6] Moberly, R. W. L. "Whose Justice? Which Righteousness? The Interpretation of Isaiah 5:18," *VT* 51, Fasc. 1 (2001): 55-68.

and righteousness like an ever-flowing stream.
(Amos 5:21-24; *cf* Mic 6:6-8)

In sum, the implications of *mishpat ve-tzedakah* for examining the prophetically influenced priestly scribal perspective on political economy cannot be overstated. Their pairing not only gives insight into this community's idealized experience of God but helps delimit right socioeconomic relationships among human beings. Such is the model that informs the socio-economic vision of the world that might be. It is tied to the concept of the divine image in Genesis 1 and what it means to be created in the *imago Dei*. According to this perspective, if the Deity is revealed to be a god of steadfast lovingkindness manifested through justice and righteousness, who establishes this model for proper human behavior, then intercourse with any other god would necessarily affirm some other sort of paradigm. By rejecting idols along with their alternative moral and ethical frameworks, one is faced with the scriptural demands of justice and righteousness (*mishpat ve-tzedakah*) and the necessary balance required of their pairing.

Conclusion

With the biblical measuring line of justice and righteousness stretched over national and global landscapes, the question remains whether a political economy that neglects the fundamental biblical principles of compassion and action on behalf of the poor is in any way sustainable. For example, it is the world's poor—those who do not over-produce or over-consume—who will be the first to suffer the dire effects of the climate crisis. From a biblical perspective, a social economy that supports a wealthy elite whose resources facilitate ongoing manipulation of the system at the expense of its socioeconomic base sews the seeds of its own demise, carrying the innocent along with them, just as Amos's judgment against the elite of Israel unfairly affected the lives of the poor as well.

Those for whom the Bible is relevant understand that hearing its words through the lens of prophetic concerns is essential. While ancient and modern worldviews differ, the prophetic perspective remains as relevant as ever. In response to a question once raised at a past OCABS Symposium concerning how to actualize the biblical perspective in the contemporary world, clearly the dominant prophetic call for steadfast love of neighbor (which includes people we may not know or even like) must be manifested in justice and righteousness, resounding in our biblical studies and in our homilies. The scathing self-critique that keeps us honest and authentic must rise above the lauds of Israel's inglorious kings and questionable heroes. It must also transcend the triumphalist perspectives of the restored community in the books of Chronicles, Ezra-Nehemiah, Haggai, and Zechariah, where the returnees to Jerusalem appear not to have learned the lesson. The acquisition of wealth and power in and of itself is less important than one's attitudes toward it, but trusting in it for deliverance is idolatrous, let alone falling far short of the command to sell all one has and give to the poor (Lk 18:22).

Chapter 6
The Trouble with Temples

Thus says the Lord, "Are you the one to build me a house to live in? I have not lived in a house since the day I brought up the people of Israel from Egypt to this day, but I have been moving about in a tent and a tabernacle." (2 Sam 7:4-6)

Do not trust in these lying words: "The temple of the Lord, the temple of the Lord, the temple of the Lord." (Jer 7:4)

Christian churches and cathedrals are among the grandest and most elaborate structures on earth. Roman Catholic houses of worship are the tallest and most ubiquitous, while Protestant mega-churches are huge, sprawling auditoriums built lower to the ground. And temples throughout the Orthodox world are no less humble. The recently consecrated National Cathedral in Bucharest, known as the People's Salvation Cathedral (*Catedrala Mântuirii Neamului*), covers nearly 65,000 square feet in area, with the tip of its cross rising more than 440 feet in the air. Belgrade's Temple to St. Sava (*Hram Svetog Save*), under construction since 1935, is relatively shorter and smaller in area, but is equally impressive to behold. Far from exhausting the list, the Primary Church of the Russian Armed Forces (*Glavnyy khram Vooruzhyonnykh sil Rossii*), dedicated to the Resurrection of Christ in honor of Russia's military victory over the Nazis in WWII, is the largest and most ironic Orthodox mega-structure in the world. Consecrated in 2020, two years before Russia's illicit invasion of Ukraine was proclaimed a Holy War by Patriarch Kirill of Moscow, it is arguably one of the world's greatest obscenities.

There are dozens of other grandiose and ornate Orthodox temples that could be mentioned, but these few examples are enough to illustrate why the prophetic perspective might be critical of their grand ostentatiousness for the glory of God. Building a worthy house for God—a place where worshipers

can offer due adoration, thanksgiving, and praise—may seem a
reasonable thing to do, but not everyone is so impressed. A
perennial criticism is the exorbitant cost that goes into
constructing such massive monuments within the world's most
impoverished nations. These colossal edifices are often built at
great expense, with little thought to the diversion of wealth away
from the physical needs of ordinary people. Romania, for
example, one of the poorest nations in the EU and the recipient
of a huge IMF bailout in 2009, provided millions of euros for
the construction of Orthodox churches throughout the country;
that is, until public funds were diverted to completion of the
Romania's new national cathedral. According to recent press
reports, only about a quarter of the construction expenses have
been subsidized by private donors, corporations, and outside
interests, with the rest from public funds directed to the church
as permitted by Romanian law. Citizens are generally
appreciative of the new edifice but would like to see greater
fiscal responsibility on the part of their government toward the
building of needed hospitals and roads.

Another problem is the frequent clandestine relationships that
exist among political and religious officials that continue beyond
the 1989 regime change to cultivate a façade of artificial
religiosity and feed suspicions of corruption. Recently, high-
level corruption involving Archbishop Teodosie (Petrescu) of
Tomis, Romania, was revealed and the case has been sent to
trial as of this writing. The archbishop was filmed allegedly
bribing a wealthy businessman to channel public money to his
archdiocese; however, it has been reported that the corruption
extends even higher. According to the *Recorder*
(www.recorder.ro), an independent Romanian news
organization founded by investigative journalists in 2017, the
Romanian National Anticorruption Directorate began
investigating a covert arrangement of businessmen, politicians
and upper-level prelates of the Church to cooperate in the
construction and rehabilitation of churches with public money,

operating with the blessing of the Patriarch himself, whom the network's operatives apparently refer to as "the Great White."[1]

The situation in Romania is just an example. Corruption between Church and state throughout the Balkans and Russia is an unholy tradition that surprises no who has been paying attention. It calls to mind the Gospel account of Jesus overturning the tables of the money changers in the temple courtyard, and it is easy to imagine that these modern-day temples function in a manner not so far removed from that of temples in antiquity. Temples in any era are built with the putative idea of honoring deities with lavish places to dwell, maintained by functionaries charged with ensuring an abiding divine presence; however, it is also the case that worship inevitably becomes stagnant, hollow, and lax as an emphasis on architectural and ritual structures overshadow moral, ethical, and spiritual considerations. Imagining that God smiles down upon our lavish temples while the poor are starving for food is an insidious form of idolatry. According to the prophetically influenced priestly scribes struggling to come to grips with the destruction of their temple, Yahweh destroyed the house they had built—not that there was anything wrong with the edifice itself, but those who had placed their trust in it had all but forgotten the Deity for whom it was built. From the exile in far-off Babylon, Ezekiel affirms that Yahweh has left the building in which his name should dwell (see 2 Kgs 23:27). A brief word about the nature and function of temples in the ancient Near East should help sharpen the contrast with the prophetically influenced priestly critique of the Jerusalem temple.

Temples in the Ancient World

Migrating through Mesopotamian wilderness, nomadic and semi-nomadic pastoralists experienced numinous encounters that likely provoked meaningful reactions. Phenomenologists of religion refer to such experiences as *mysterium tremendum et*

---

[1] https://recorder.ro/clanul-marelui-alb/?mc_cid=5debd9f6d0&mc_eid=cd1f92f96c

fascinans, the mystery that threatens one's mortal being, yet exerts an irresistible attraction by a promise of ultimate fulfilment.[2] This dynamic ambivalent response to an appearance of the sacred (*hierophany*) is illustrated by Moses' encounter with God on Mount Horeb:

> Moses was keeping the flock of his father-in-law Jethro, the priest of Midian; he led his flock beyond the wilderness, and came to Horeb, the mountain of God. There the angel of the Lord appeared to him in a flame of fire out of a bush. He looked and saw the bush was burning but was not consumed. Then Moses said, "I must turn aside and look at this great sight and see why the bush is not burned up." When the Lord saw that he had turned aside to see, God called to him out of the bush, "Moses, Moses!" And he said, "Here I am." Then he said, "Do not come any no closer. Remove the sandals from your feet, for the place on which you are standing is holy ground." He then said, "I am the God of your father, the God of Abraham, the God of Isaac, and the God of Jacob." And Moses hid his face, for he was afraid to look at God. (Exod 3:1-6)

Extraordinary events—such as hostile encounters with aggressive tribes, the strike of a lightning bolt, or the death of a loved one—would be remembered and perhaps commemorated by piling a heap of stones. While anthropologists continue to debate the function of phenomena such as dolmens and menhirs,[3] most agree that the behavior is a universal human response to natural forces and events perceived to be extraordinary. Whatever the motivation for leaving behind a remembrance of the event, any fear or

---

[2] The term means "the mystery that evokes an ambivalent simultaneous response of fear and attraction. It began with Rudolf Otto's 1917 book *Das Heilege* (The Sacred) and was formulated in its present form by Mircea Eliade.

[3] Dolmens, usually described as table-shaped megaliths, and menhirs, which are large upright stones, are prehistoric structures found across all of Europe and into western Asia. Major dolmen fields along the Jordan rift include Rasm Harbush, Damiyeh, and al-Mureighat, all of which may be explored virtually at www.virtualworldproject.org.

insecurity associated with the experience could be mitigated simply by moving on.

The adaptation to settled life that accompanied the development of agriculture raised other sorts of fears and insecurities, specifically concerning forces of weather and climate. Violent storms were no longer a temporary calamity hunters could weather by seeking shelter in a cave. For settled populations, floods, drought, and famine seriously threatened food and water supplies for entire seasons, sometimes necessitating relocation. Gods of weather, fertility, and death predominated and had to be appeased. As a result, the invention and proliferation of ceramic technology, which developed concurrently with agriculture, saw the production of altars, libation bowls, figurines, and other items for cultic use, domestic and public. As populations increased and became stratified and more complex, the public display of religion expanded and became formalized. The increased power and authority of groups who possessed the specialized knowledge to approach and appease the gods served to distance the inner workings of religion from ordinary people. Although public open-air sanctuaries are attested in the material record, the discovery of household deities indicates that domestic religion continued alongside it, most notably in association with family burials.

The development of large city-states in the fourth-millennium BCE included the construction of temples, sacred houses that connected heaven and earth through the mediation of kings and priests. Early temples in Sumer consisted of a single rectangular chamber located near or adjoining the palace. By the end of the third millennium BCE, temples became larger and more complex, with stairs ascending to platforms where gods could grant audience and be appeased. Commonly known as *ziggurats*, these structures facilitated intercourse between the earth and the heavens so that respective expectations could be mediated, and world brought into alignment with the orderliness of the cosmos.[4] Persuading divine powers to remain nearby required attention to the things that would compel them to remain, such as the construction of a suitable dwelling place, as indicated by the Akkadian word for temple, *bit*, literally, "house."

In addition to uncovering the material remains of temple architecture, archaeologists have recovered hundreds of thousands of cuneiform texts inscribed on clay tablets, as well as artifacts including stelae, figurines, cylinder seals, and vases, which provide insight into Mesopotamian religion. As city-states emerged, the temple took on responsibilities beyond merely providing an arena for public worship. Because a polity's dependence on the benevolence of gods was paramount, it bore the theo-political necessity of legitimizing rulers (and in rare cases delegitimizing them), providing divine support and guiding them in the regulation and enforcement of laws. In addition, the temple served an economic role, controlling vast tracts of agricultural land, determining the start of planting season, stockpiling harvests, and regulating the distribution of grain.

Of course, what is a temple without its priesthood? These highly trained specialists represented various levels and classes according to function, often based on possessing the proper pedigree. High priests were charged with the perilous responsibility of entering the holiest area (*qodesh ha-qodeshim*, later the Greco-Roman *cella*) to approach the image of the god (or gods) with humble petitions and offerings of sacrificial gifts sufficiently worthy to seal the deal. Responsibilities for prescribed acts of adoration and worship were distributed among a complex network of lesser male and female functionaries, who sang hymns of praise, recited petitions, performed ritual dancing, or attended to menial tasks required for maintaining regular temple functions.

---

[4] The desire for an orderly correspondence between the divine and earthly realms is reflected in the line from the Lord's Prayer, "… thy will be done on earth as it is in heaven").

In sum, the temple operated alongside the palace as a guarantor of ongoing social and economic stability. Its access to the formidable powers that created and ordered the cosmos through the recitation of myths and proper enactments of rituals, carried the promise of peace and security for the city and its inhabitants whether they remained consciously awareness of it or not. At any rate, any sudden appearance of danger presented an urgent reminder to call upon the gods with renewed and exuberant sincerity.[5] According to the prophets who sought to explain the destruction of the Jerusalem temple, remembering the Lord had turned out to be too little too late.

The Temple in the Hebrew Bible

First Kings 6:1 states that construction of the Temple began 480 years after the Israelites' exodus from the land of Egypt, a tantalizing cue were it not for the fact that no one knows the date of the exodus, let alone the origin of the story.[6] While this foundational narrative of the people Israel may preserve a kernel of Levitical priestly memory of a leader named Moses (an Egyptian name associated with water), there is no way to determine when it might have occurred. In addition, the number 480 is suspicious, given it is the product of two highly

---

[5] Excavations at et-Tell/Bethsaida revealed hastily built modifications to the city wall as the forces of the Assyrian leader Tiglath-Pileser III approached. Of all the basalt stones needed to help fortify the wall, we noticed one stone had been set aside and planted upright as a stela alongside the end of the wall nearest the city gate, suggesting it may have been consecrated as a votive offering appealing to the city's moon god patron (Yarikh, probably) for added protection from above.

[6] There is nary a shred of historical extra-biblical evidence that the Exodus as recounted in the Bible actually occurred. The idea of 2.5 million people migrating en masse from Egypt to Cannan while leaving no evidence of cultural disruption in the material remains at the point of arrival renders it all but impossible. The Bible cites the exodus of 603,550 Hebrew men (Num 1:46), along with their families and servants, which marching 50 abreast and allowing ten feet between ranks for carts and animals would form a column stretching roughly 95 miles long This would be sustained for forty years with accumulations of birth. Having said that, the late Israeli intellectual, Nahum Sarna, observed the unlikelihood that a people would situate their very origins in slavery and then continue to iterate and reiterate how unfaithful they were to God.

symbolic biblical numbers (12 x 40), making it likely the number was not intended to be factual.[7] Moreover, if one adds 480 years to the year 960 BCE, which is the year most biblical scholars calculate for the building of the temple, we arrive around the year 1440 BCE, an untenable conclusion given that Thutmose III of Egypt (18th Dynasty) had complete military and administrative control over Canaan at that time. Moreover, there is no sign of the Egyptians in the conquest narratives of Joshua and Judges. Outside the Bible, the origin and specifications of any temple in an early Israelite kingdom remains lost to history.

This is not to say that no Judahite temple sat atop Mount Moriah—the present-day site of the al-Aqsa mosque compound and its iconic golden-domed Haram al-Sharif—nor that this temple was destroyed during the Babylonian incursions of the early sixth-century BCE.[8] What is not known from archaeology or any other source is when the temple edifice was first built, rebuilt, or renovated (e.g., 2 Chr 24:4-14). Fortunately, these questions need not detain us. What is important is the horrific impact the destruction of the temple had for the sixth-century BCE kingdom of Judah. The fact that Yahweh's house lay in ruins must have led Judahites to conclude that the Babylonian god Marduk (or the Edomites' Qos) were stronger than Yahweh; for the might of gods was evidenced through the victories of their earthly client kings. However, there was one circle of priests unwilling to accept such a proposition. Heeding the words of certain prophets like Ezekiel and Jeremiah, they reasoned that if Yahweh's house lay in ruins then only Yahweh himself could have brought it about. This conviction left them with the perplexing question of why it would be so, but it did

---

[7] With the conviction that God works in ordered increments of history, the Deuteronomistic writer of the seventh-century BCE appears to be spotlighting the dedication of the temple by situating it at the center of history, that is, somewhere between the foundational narrative of the Exodus and his own present day.

[8] Biblical scholar Richard E. Friedman makes a convincing argument that the temple was destroyed by the Edomites; see https://www.academia.edu/45034619/The_Destruction_of_the_First_Jerusalem_Temple.

not take long for them to arrive at the answer. They took up a triumphalist record of their past—one that otherwise would have ended up in the dustbin of history alongside the boastful annals of all other ancient kingdoms—and reworked it to produce one of the most scathing collective self-examinations human beings have ever produced. Unfortunately, most Jewish and Christian readers choose to focus on the triumphalist layer of the narrative, failing to realize Hosea's words to the royal and priestly leaders of Israel that all the structures of power—including the house of God—will be torn down, and that "this judgment pertains to you!" (Hos 5:1).

As we have seen, the two-stage literary composition of the Deuteronomistic history retains earlier triumphalist materials concerning the temple but overlays it with a post-destruction retrospective that seeks to answer the troubling question of what had gone so terribly wrong. The pivotal point toward the disaster is easily seen in 2 Kgs 22:29-30. There one can imagine the writer in shock and sadness taking up his pen to fashion an addendum to the triumphalist Josianic scroll that would make sense of the unexpected tragedy that had just occurred:

> In his [Josiah's] days, Pharaoh Necho, king of Egypt, went up to the king of Assyria who was encamped at the Euphrates River. King Josiah went to head him off, but when Pharaoh Necho met him at Megiddo, he killed him. His servants carried him dead in a chariot from Megiddo, brought him to Jerusalem, and laid him in his tomb. (vv. 29-30)

Under peaceful circumstances, the story of King Josiah and all his deeds would have ended with formulaic words of praise; however, news of his unexpected death required a theological explanation:

> But still the Lord did not turn from the fierceness of his great wrath by which his anger was kindled against Judah because of all the provocations with which Manasseh had provoked him. The Lord said, "I will remove Judah also out of my sight, as I have removed Israel, and I will reject this city that I have chosen,

Jerusalem, and the house of which I said, 'My name shall be there.'" (2 Kgs 23:26-27)

If Josiah was so great a leader for renovating the temple, promulgating the Law of Moses, and centralizing exclusive worship of Yahweh in Jerusalem, why the sudden mention of Josiah's grandfather, King Manasseh, portrayed in the Bible as the wickedest king ever to occupy the throne of Judah?

It is almost certainly historical that Josiah was felled by an Egyptian arrow as he sought to thwart the Pharaoh from allying with Assyrian forces along the Euphrates. Perhaps he was hoping to score points with the neo-Babylonians. At any rate, his unexpected death required the writer to scramble for an explanation that would make sense of the good king's demise and the tragic chain of events that followed, so he chose to implicate Josiah's grandfather, Manasseh. The son and successor of King Hezekiah, Manasseh reigned fifty-five years—longer than any other Israelite or Judahite king. During the entirety of his reign, he successively negotiated his kingdom's vassalage to the Assyrian empire. The stability and diplomacy of his lengthy reign offer much to commend him, but he is defamed and scapegoated by the biblical writer as a heavier counterbalance to the righteousness of King Josiah. Manasseh provided the literary justification for divine judgment upon Judah, overshadowing all of Josiah's Deuteronomistic reforms.

The reign of Josiah and the fall of Jerusalem, which took within a span of just three decades, offers a classical "best of times / worst of times" scenario. These tumultuous years were witnessed firsthand by the prophet Jeremiah who, bereft of Josiah's support, suffered miserably at the hands of the Jerusalem officials poisoned by Zion theology. A misguided conviction arising from remembrance of Jerusalem's deliverance from destruction by the Assyrians a little over a century earlier, Zion theology asserted that God would unconditionally protect their city from the Babylonians as well (2 Kgs 19:34).[9]

Of course, Jeremiah proves to be correct, but being right does not always go over well. Like all true prophets, Jeremiah's prescience is based not on clairvoyance, but on the ability to read the "writing on the wall" (Dan 5:25); that is, rightly interpreting the signs of the times. Anticipating the impending disaster, Jeremiah offers his answer to the question of why things would soon go terribly wrong. Because his words are too important to abridge, the passage is rendered here in its entirety. Standing at the gate of the temple, he proclaims:

> "Hear the word of the Lord, all Judahites who enter these gates to worship the Lord. Thus says the Lord of heavenly powers, the God of Israel: "Amend your ways and your doings and I will dwell with you in this place, but do not trust in these lying words, 'The temple of the Lord, the temple of the Lord, the temple of the Lord are these.' But if you thoroughly amend your ways and your doings; and if you thoroughly enforce justice between a man and his neighbor; if you not oppress the stranger, the orphan, and the widow, and shed not innocent blood in this place, neither walk after other gods to your detriment; then I will cause you to dwell in this place, in the land that I gave to your fathers for ever and ever.

> Behold, you trust in lying words that bring no benefit. Will you steal and murder, commit adultery and give false witness, and offer unto Baal and walk after other gods whom you have not known, and come stand before me in this house in which my name is called and say, 'We are delivered,' that you may commit all these despicable acts? Has this house in which my name is called upon become a den of thieves in your eyes? Behold I, even I, have seen it," says the Lord. (Jer 7:1-11)

---

[9] It is the case that after laying waste to Judah, Sennacherib did not breach the walls of Jerusalem, but while the Bible attributes his failure to the intervention of an angel of the Lord who struck down his army overnight (2 Kgs 19:35), the historical reason seems to be his need to retreat to defend his own capital from neo-Babylonian attack.

The contrast between the words of the sixth-century BCE prophets regarding Jerusalem and its temple, and the positive way Jerusalem and its temple are described in the pre-destruction draft of the Deuteronomistic history, and again in post-exilic texts like Haggai and Zechariah, is striking. By contrast, Jeremiah, a descendant of the northern Levitical tradition at Anatoth, along with Isaiah and Ezekiel, priests of the Jerusalem temple, describe their city as a "prostitute" and "city of blood" (Ezek 16:15-43; 22:1-12; 24:6; Jer 3:1-9).[10] In addition, the frequent prophecies *ex eventu* retrojected into biblical Israel's narrative past (Dtr[2]) have the effect of "foretelling" the future by providing reasons for how and why these kingdoms came to their respective ends.

An obvious example is the account of Solomon's construction of the palace-temple complex (1 Kings 6–8), which in its final form came to be framed by two dream visions. But why the need for a second dream, unless the first dream was somehow inadequate? A comparison of the dreams is telling. The first presents a lofty tribute to Solomon and his desire for wisdom, something one would expect from a loyal royal scribe:

> And now, O Lord my God, you have made your servant king in place of my father David, although I am only a little child; I do not know how to go out or come in. And your servant stands amid the people you have chosen, a great people so numerous they cannot be numbered or counted. Give your servant, therefore, an understanding mind to govern your people, able to discern between good and evil, for who can govern this great people of yours? (1 Kgs 3:7-9)

However, Solomon's wisdom collapses on several fronts as he succumbs to idolatry, despotism, and greed. The post-destruction revision not only demonstrates the eventual failure of Israel's leadership, but reflects a critique of the temple, foreshadowing its destruction with the use of conditional language—an outcome already in the editor's rearview mirror:

---

[10] See for example, Isa 1:21; Ezek 16:35-52; 22:2; and 24:6.

> If you turn aside from following me, you or your children, and do not keep my commandments and my statutes that I have set before you but go and serve other gods and worship them, then I will cut Israel off from the land that I have given them; and the house that I have consecrated for my name I will cast out of my sight; and Israel will become a proverb and a taunt among all peoples. This house will become a heap of ruins; everyone passing by it will be astonished, and will hiss; and they will say, 'Why has the Lord done such a thing to this land and to this house?' Then they will say, 'Because they have forsaken the Lord their God, who brought their ancestors out of the land of Egypt, and embraced other gods, worshipping them and serving them; therefore, the Lord has brought this disaster upon them.'" (1 Kgs 9:6-9)

From the prophetic perspective, divine displeasure not only provides a rational explanation for the destruction of Yahweh's house but goes further in spotlighting the misplaced trust that Judahites had invested in works of their hands. To stand in the court of the temple and say this is "the temple of the Lord, the temple of the Lord, the temple of the Lord" is to proclaim a lie, according to Jeremiah; for the Lord does not dwell in a house in an unclean land persisting in gross iniquity.

The notion that God is not restricted to a house made with hands is reflected in Nathan's admonition to King David, which asserts that the Lord dwells among nomadic and pastoral peoples living in tents in the wilderness and not in a fixed house made with hands:

> Since the day I brought up the people of Israel from Egypt to this day I have not lived in a house but have been moving about in a tent and a tabernacle. Wherever I have moved about among the people of Israel, did I ever say to any of the tribal leaders "Why have you not built me a house of cedar?" (2 Sam 7:5-7)

Of course, the biblical writers must acknowledge the historical reality of the temple, which regardless of when it was built, existed in their own day. They certainly could not write it out of history; but notice that the quiet part has been stated clearly and aloud, namely that "the Most High does not dwell in a house made with hands," a position Solomon seems to acknowledge as well:

> The house that I am about to build will be great, for our God is greater than other gods. But who is able to build him a house, since heaven, even highest heaven, cannot contain him? Who am I to build a house for him except as a place to make offerings before him? (1 Kgs 2:5-6)

Apparently, the scribes deemed it inappropriate to attribute the building of the temple to David, "a man of battle who has shed blood" (1 Chr 28:3). Instead, they attribute the task to King Solomon, who takes advantage of the regional peace wrought by his father. Solomon builds the temple, but also takes the opportunity to construct a lavish palace for himself (1 Kgs 7:1; 2 Chronicles 2:1, 12). Construction of the temple is said to begin in the fourth year of his reign, in the second month (*Ziv*), and is completed in the eleventh year of his reign, in the eighth month of the year (*Bul*), roughly seven years in all (1 Kgs 6:37-38). By contrast, Solomon spends thirteen years fashioning his own palace (1 Kgs 7:1), which Josephus (*Ant.* 5.1) and most other commentators attribute to having less concern for his own dwelling than building a house for Yahweh,[11] but could just as easily indicate the opposite, namely that he cares more for his own dwelling than for God's.

The longer period could also be due to the elaborate dimensions of each aspect of the palace complex. The temple dimensions are roughly 180 feet by 90 feet, by 50 feet high, while Solomon's palace is described as having several halls that take up even more real estate (1 Kgs 7:1-8). The Hall of the Forest was roughly 150 feet long by 75 feet wide by 45 feet high; the Hall of Columns was 75 feet long by 45 feet wide. There is also the Hall of Justice, the throne room where cases are adjudicated, the dimensions of which are not provided. Solomon's own quarters are located in another court behind the

---

[11] *Ant.* 5.1

Hall of Judgment, with a similar house for his wife, a princess of Egypt, and presumably other quarters for his thousand wives and concubines.

Finally, the critique of the temple is revived in the Hellenistic period in lines from the latter chapters of Isaiah, which contrasts temple worship with the need for personal piety:

> Thus says the Lord:
> Heaven is my throne,
> and the earth is my footstool;
> so what kind of house could you build for me,
> what sort of place for me to rest?
> All these things my hand has made,
> so all these things are mine,
> says the Lord.
> But this is the one to whom I will look,
> to the humble and contrite in spirit
> who trembles at my word. (Isa 66:1-2)

It is also survives in Stephen's critique of the rebuilt temple in the book of Acts:

> For the Most High does not dwell in houses made with hands [ἀλλ' οὐχ ὁ ὕψιστος ἐν χειροποιήτοις κατοικεῖ]. As the prophet says, "Heaven is my throne, and the earth is my footstool. What kind of house will you build for me? says the Lord, or what is the place of my rest? Did not my hand make all these things?" (Acts 7:48-50; citing Isa 66:1-2)

Thus, it is the temple—and every temple since—that joins the ranks of human-wrought institutions serving as illusory bulwarks against fear and insecurity. As repositories of misplaced trust in the works of the hands, they are idols as long as they help the worshiper to feel good about not committing to the work of the demands of the Gospel to fear God and feed and clothe one another.

Conclusion

The biblical prophets were bold in their critique of temple worship. Certainly, it was not the temple itself that posed a problem, but the lack of a proper attitude on the part of king and priests and people that led to perfunctory and cavalier behavior in relation to it, especially in terms of idolatry, immorality, and social injustice. One might well acknowledge that God is too big to fit in any sort of house, or that it would make no difference to God how large and ornate such a house might be. But the default mode seems to be that somehow the more elaborate the temple, the more it will hide the sins of the people from their own view, providing a false sense of well-being that fails to deliver a nation in times of trouble. By contrast, the proper attitude toward worship, sometimes expressed as a circumcision of the heart (Deut 10:16; 30:6; Jer 4:4; cf. 1QpHab 11; 4Q184; Rom 2:28-29; 1 Cor 6:19), places responsibility for right worship in the heart of the worshiper.

Chapter 7
The Trouble with Prophets

Then Moses, the servant of the Lord, died there in the land of Moab at the word of the Lord. He was buried in a valley in the land of Moab, across from Beth-peor, and no one knows his burial place to this day. Moses was a hundred twenty years old when he died. His eye was not dimmed nor his life force diminished. (Deut 34:5-7)

After the man of God had eaten food and drink, they saddled a donkey belonging to the prophet who had brought him back. And as he went away, a lion met him on the road and killed him. His body was thrown in the road, and the donkey stood beside it. The lion also stood beside the body. (1 Kgs 13:23-24)

It is noteworthy that the prophetic guild can be just as critical of itself as it is of the other institutions covered in this book. Prophetic literature's condemnation of false prophets is commonplace (Jer 14:14; 23:16; Ezek 22:28), but the frequent minimization and even negation of its own protagonists is enlightening. True biblical prophets capture the attention of readers and hearers with discomforting speech and bizarre actions that direct them toward the divine Word, raising the possibility that these dynamic messengers would be exalted above their due. This is the main reason Islam forbids depictions of the Prophet Muhammad, thereby preserving the doctrine of God's unique oneness (*tawid*) by eliminating the possibility that the mortal Prophet might be venerated or even idolized.

The concept is securely rooted in scripture. The book of Deuteronomy assures readers that no one knows where Moses is buried to this day (Deut 34:6), but why would the writer provide so random a literary datum except to admonish readers that searching it out for the purpose of erecting some monumental tombstone or shrine would be a misguided thing to do. Certainly, such guidance has not deterred people from trying. Today the Franciscan order's Memorial Church of Moses (*Maqam Nabi Musa*) sits high atop Mt. Nebo directly over the remains of a fourth-century monastery. According to the travel account of the fourth-century pilgrim Egeria, the monks claimed that an angel had revealed to them that their monastery had been constructed directly above Moses' grave, despite contradicting the biblical account placing Moses' burial in the valley below. Anti-idolatry efforts aside, people always manage to find a way to slip around scriptural guardrails, even if it means co-opting the witness of an angel.

Other examples of Jewish, Christian, and Muslim veneration of prophets include a 14th-century, white-domed mosque perched high atop a peak at Petra, built to mark the traditional burial place of Moses' brother Aaron, which Islam considers to be a prophet (Sura Maryam, 53). There is also the celebrated Tomb of the Prophets—specifically Haggai, Zechariah, and Malachi—perched on the upper western slope of the Mount of Olives overlooking East Jerusalem, which archaeology reveals dates no earlier than the first century BCE. Perhaps sufficient for making the point are the multiple burial sites for the prophet Isaiah, who apparently lies buried near the village of Silwan, along the Wadi Kidron just south of Jerusalem; or near the site of the eradicated Palestinian village of Dayshum, along the Wadi Dishon in the Galilee; or in the Tomb of Isaiah, located in the Imamzadeh Ismail complex in the former Jewish Quarter of Isfahan, Iran.

Not to be ignored are dozens of putative tombs and shrines of other biblical figures scattered throughout Palestine and beyond. The fact that most of these are fictional or legendary characters does not deter the need for setting up tombs and monuments for their fictive bodies. Even the so-called Righteous Lot—the despicable father willing to throw his daughters out the door to be raped, who according to Gen 19:29, is rescued from Sodom only by dint of the fact he happens to be the nephew of God's friend Abraham—yes, even the fictional Lot—has his own burial site at Bani Na'im, a Palestinian village located roughly five miles east of Hebron.[1]

The phenomenon of prophecy in all its many forms is perhaps the most salient aspect of revealed religion in that it channels direct communication from the divine realm to the human world. Whether serving as a legitimizing organ of the royal court or arising spontaneously in the form of charismatic visionaries in times of calamity, prophecy runs deep and wide throughout the history of the ancient Near East and is so varied that specialized language evolved to accommodate its many forms and variations. The famous Mari texts, which date to the first half of the eighteenth-century BCE,[2] mention several types of prophetic intermediaries whose functions include religious consultation, performance, oratory, and ecstatic abandon in altered states of consciousness,[3] traces of which may be found in the Hebrew Bible.

Although these prophetic modes of communication are present in biblical literature, a concerted effort to transform them into a more uniform, less bizarre channel of purpose is evident. Nevertheless, the reader finds an array of bizarre,

---

[1] I am at a loss to understand how the writer of 2 Pet 2:7 deems Lot righteous simply because he was distressed by the conduct of the lawless townsmen when his willingness to surrender his daughters to be raped is equally depraved. Some Protestant Christians explain that Lot was deemed righteous by Abraham's righteousness in the way that Christ's faithfulness (*pistis Christou*; see, for example, Gal 2:16) redeems the sinner, but diminishing the unique efficacy of Christ's salvific grace seems misguided, if not heretical.

[2] Since the early 1930's, the site of the ancient city of Mari, in northern Syria, has yielded over 25,000 tablets, mostly in Akkadian, comprising some 15,000 texts from its royal archives, providing valuable insight into the sociocultural, religious, and legal practices of the region, especially for the Amorites, for whom this great city served as its capital for about the last 250 years of its roughly 1,000-year history (ca. 2800–1760 BCE).

[3] In one of the Mari texts, an ecstatic prophetic (*muhhu*) stands before the king and the people eating a raw lamb as a prophetic sign; see M. Anbar, "Trois Documents de la Collection Leo Perutz," IOS 6, 59-63. For general coverage of prophecy in the ANE, see Martti Nissenen, *Prophecy in its Ancient Near Eastern Context: Mesopotamian, Biblical, and Arabian Perspectives* (Atlanta, SBL, 2000); see also, "Prophecy" in ABD, vol. 5 (New York: Doubleday, 1992).

sometimes disturbing ways the divine Word is communicated: Elisha floats an iron ax head on water (2 Kgs 6:1-7) and overthrows a foreign king (2 Kgs 8:7-15); Amos sees metaphoric visions that portend the nation's utter doom; Hosea weds a woman of whoredom; Jeremiah walks around Jerusalem waving a dirty loincloth in the faces of its inhabitants (Jer 13:1-11); Isaiah parades around naked for three years (Isa 20:2-4); and so on. One of the most unsettling examples of all is Ezekiel, an exiled priest and prophet, whose life is expressed through a barrage of extraordinary visions and aberrant actions.

To be sure, one cannot speak of the prophets without using the language of action, which should come as no surprise given that Yahweh as a God of action.[4] One only has to take note of the number of times the Lord tells Elijah to go, followed by the words "and Elijah went." Whether wildly ecstatic in the manner of their ancient Near Eastern counterparts or not, biblical prophecy is never about the prophets themselves, but about the divine word expressed through their actions, utterances, and visions. Despite the fact that some prophets may have attracted certain "schools" of disciples, there appears to be no sort of hero worship or celebrity status accorded them. On the contrary, there is an observable tendency for the institution of prophecy to stay out of its own way lest it obstruct the hearing of the divine word they are driven to reveal.

Prophetic Self-Negation in the Deuteronomistic History

An essential component of the prophetical priestly perspective runs like a crimson thread through the Deuteronomistic history, a corpus known traditionally as the Former Prophets. As we saw earlier, it tells a story that begins with Israel's triumphal

---

[4] Abraham Heschel's classic work *The Prophets* (2 vols. New York: Harper Collins, 1962; Rpt. Harper Perennial Modern Classics, 2001), still relevant after more than sixty years, emphasizes the ultimate humanity of the prophets by associating their psychological motivations as "sympathy with the divine pathos" (Vol. 1, p. 26).

entrance into the Promised Land and ends with its violent expulsion from it. In some ways, scholarly departure from the traditional term Former Prophets is unfortunate, for although Dtr[1] once served as a chronicle of kings, its post-destruction revision presents them as tragically flawed, dismal failures judged and harangued by Israel's true warriors, the biblical prophets, operating under the command of the divine King.

The constellation of pegs upon which the overall Deuteronomistic narrative is draped is a series of foreshadowing prophecies *ex eventu* strewn throughout the sermons of Moses, the prophet and prototype of subsequent prophets that include the "prophet like me" in Deut 18:15.[5] This includes prophetic expectations for Israelite kings, anticipating royal vices like Solomon's polygamous idolatry, or virtues like Josiah's observance of the law.

> When you have come into the land that the Lord your has given you and have taken possession of it and settled in it, and you say, "I will set a king over me, like all the nations that are around me," you may indeed set over you a king whom the Lord your God will choose. You may set one of your own people as king over you, but you are not permitted to put a foreigner over you, someone who is not of your own community." Even so, he must not acquire many horses for himself or return the people to Egypt in order to acquire more horses, since the Lord has said to you, 'You must never return that way again." And he must not acquire many wives for himself or else his heart will turn away; also silver and gold he must not acquire in great quantity for himself. When he has taken the throne of his kingdom, he shall have a copy of this law written for him in the presence of the Levitical priests. It shall remain with him and he shall read in it all the days of his

---

[5] The unnamed prophet like Moses almost certainly refers to someone in the Deuteronomist's own time, for which the most likely candidate is Jeremiah, an opinion that can be traced as far back as the 15th C Portuguese Jewish sage Isaac Abravanel (or Abarbanel). See W. L. Holladay, "The Background of Jeremiah's Self-Understanding: Moses, Samuel, and Psalm 22," *JBL* 83 (1964), 153-64; see also, C. R. Seitz, "The Prophet Moses and the Canonical Shape of Jeremiah, " *ZAW* 101 (1989), 3-27.

life, so that he may learn to fear the LORD his God, diligently observing all the words of this law and these statutes, neither exalting himself above other members of the community nor turning aside from the commandment, either to the right or to the left, so that he and his descendants may reign long over his kingdom in Israel. (Deut 17:14-20)

The Deuteronomist reflects a bias in asserting prophetic status above kings. Samuel, a judge and priestly functionary,[6] is a prophet with the divine authority to anoint both Saul (10:1) and David (16:13).[7] Similarly, the Lord commissions Elijah to anoint Jehu (1 Kgs 19:16), a task that falls to his disciple Elisha (2 Kgs 9:1-10). Moreover, prophets boldly confront kings with oracles of divine judgment and their consequences. A "man of God" (*ish ha-elohim*) from Judah confronts Jeroboam (1 Kgs 13:1-10); Elijah confronts Ahab (1 Kgs 22:20-24); and Jehu receives prophetic judgment for not shutting down the shrines of Jeroboam (2 Kgs 10:28-31). Finally, although not exhaustively, translation of the prophetic spirit from Elijah to Elisha serves as the major link in the prophetic conduit connecting Moses with the unnamed sixth-century BCE "prophet like me" (Deut 18:15),[8] providing the interpretive lens for the entire Deuteronomistic perspective asserting that the line of true biblical prophets has always been Israel's highest and best line of defense. Dtr[2]'s reason for the fall of Jerusalem, as we

---

[6] Although Samuel performs some priestly functions in the Deuteronomistic history, he appears to lack Levitical ancestry and is nowhere explicitly called a priest. By contrast, the Chronicler accords him Levitical lineage (1 Chr 6:7-13); see "Samuel," in *ABD*, V. 954-57.

[7] The Bible occasionally accords the title of prophet to unlikely people, most notably Abraham (Gen 20:7), Miriam (15:20), and Deborah (Judg 4:4), however Samuel is the earliest figure since Moses to be recast in the prophetic role as it is classically understood, namely as one who speaks with authority in the name of God. The editorial note in 1 Sam 9:9, that the prophet (*nabi*) was once known as a seer (*hozeh*), may reflect an attempt to bring Samuel into the circle of classical prophets.

[8] The likely identification of Jeremiah with the prophet like Moses can be traced as far back as Isaac Abravanel (or Abarbanel), a 15th C Portuguese Jewish sage. See W. L. Holladay, "The Background of Jeremiah's Self-Understanding: Moses, Samuel, and Psalm 22," *JBL* 83 (1964), 153-64; see also, C. R. Seitz, "The Prophet Moses and the Canonical Shape of Jeremiah," *ZAW* 101 (1989), 3-27.

have seen all along, is that Israel had placed its trust in human institutions, specifically the monarchy, fortified cities, iron chariots, and even the temple, ignoring the word of God that issued from the mouths of the true biblical prophets. Thus, while the Deuteronomist comprises an amalgam of voices from a number of sources, including folktales, legends, priestly records, and lost annals of the kings of Israel and Judah, the definitive formative influence from oracles of doom to visions of restoration can only be called prophetical.

One of the most interesting characteristics of the prophetic perspective is its own authenticating critical self-examination, a remarkably rare thing for a social group of any era to undertake. This literary tendency finds analogy in the real-world phenomenon of ecstatic prophecy in which a shamanic-type figure attracts the attention of the community by abandoning his or her ego self to some perceived otherworldly power. Prophetic movements that result are measured by their ability to further attract and retain followers by evoking ongoing experiences of the sacred, so that what is authentic and genuine operates through and in spite of the human conduits that channel them. The imposition of personal (or collective) ego that results from a medium (or group) taking itself too seriously would be akin to throwing water upon its own fire; thus, ironically, in order to convey authentic experiences of the sacred, the human mediator needs to be there without being there, a quality that the true prophet seeks to embody.

As mentioned above, the attempt to avoid glorification of the prophet begins with Moses, whose persona is unimportant. Only what he says and does counts. He champions justice in avenging the scourged Hebrew slave and defending Jethro's daughters at the well (Exod 2:11-17), yet he is nowhere lauded as a hero. He is portrayed as fallibly human in that he lacks confidence in his own abilities and makes excuses for himself, yet he confronts Pharaoh and leads the Hebrews out of Egypt to the threshold of the Promised Land. In addition, Moses is portrayed as tirelessly patient and supremely humble (see especially Num 12:3). The only instances in which Moses is ignored, downgraded, or made to exhibit any sort of self-promotion is found in the competing Priestly tradition,[9] especially in the case of the Priestly writer's version of the "Water from the Rock" episode (Num 20:2-13). In Exod 17:1-7, which most scholars believe to be a northern tradition, Moses strikes water from a rock at Meribah as a providential agent of God to satisfy the thirsty wanderers. In the Numbers account, the prophet strikes water from the rock at Meribah and the act displeases the Most High to the point that Moses is not permitted to lead the Hebrews into the Promised Land.

The story of Moses's death (Deut 34: 5-7), in which the writer recounts the prophet's advanced age and full vigor, should be interpreted to mean that the long-suffering prophet's animating spirit (*nefesh*) did not simply wear out and fail on its own but was taken from him for no other reason than Yahweh was finished with him. That no one knows the place of his burial until this day (Deut 34:6), suggests that looking for Moses's grave anywhere on Mt. Nebo would be a futile endeavor. The search for Elijah's body in 2 Kgs 2 is an obvious parallel that reinforces the fact that one should not waste time looking for the graves of true prophets. In sum, the writer affirms the *role* of Moses as leader and lawgiver, but at the same time manipulatively minimizes the prophet's *person*. Moses's significance for the prophetic redactors is not about Moses *qua* Moses at all, but what God brings about through the agency of those whom God chooses to exploit for purposes of executing the divine will.

In the Elijah/Elisha cycle, one finds an even greater literary effort to keep the protagonist's persona out of the limelight.

---

[9] The Torah, especially Deuteronomy, and the "history" that follows appear to reflect two major competing priestly lineages, namely an older northern Levitical tradition that traces its lineage directly back to Moses, and a Zadokite priestly line that stems from Aaron. See "Levites and Priests," in *ABD*, IV. 297-310; see also William Millar, *Priesthood in Ancient Israel* (St. Louis: Chalice Press, 2001).

Obviously fashioned after the likeness of Moses, Elijah experiences a theophany on Sinai/Horeb (1 Kgs 19:11-13) and surpasses even Moses's reluctance to serve by begging to be released not only from the prophetic mission, but from his very life (v. 4). Extending neither sympathy nor comfort, the Yahweh ignores Elijah's desperate desire for death. Instead, God orders him to walk all the way back to the north, beyond his original point of departure, and carry out three tasks, including two major regime changes—one in Damascus, replacing Ben Hadad with Hazael; the other in Samaria, replacing Ahab with Jehu—after which may he enlist Elisha as his disciple and eventual successor (1 Kgs 19:15-16). It is clear from the narrative that it does not matter what Elijah himself thinks or desires; but he is fortunate enough in setting out to stumble first upon Elisha, who eventually carries out the divinely ordered *coups d'état* levied upon his master (2 Kgs 8:7-15; 9:1-10). By ordering these events in such a way, the author clearly asserts that God is ultimately pulling the strings in the ongoing drama of human history, not the prophets themselves. The prophets are God's hired guns, dispensable vehicles of the divine will.

This fact becomes especially apparent in 2 Kings 2, where Elisha closely shadows his master as God commands him to travel from Jericho to Bethel, then Gilgal and back to the Jordan River—an incredibly difficult circuit to travel and for no apparent reason other than the fact that the LORD commanded it. At each stage of the way, fifty non-Levitical priests from the formerly Levitical northern shrines re-dedicated by King Jeroboam (1 Kings 12) come out to taunt the disciple like annoying mosquitoes about the ears, telling him what he already knows to be true, namely that his master is about to be recalled from service.

Upon crossing the Jordan River, Elisha asks Elijah for a double-portion of his master's spirit, a reference to the two-thirds portion of a father's estate an eldest son would customarily expect to inherit. Elijah tells his faithful disciple that he has asked for a difficult thing, but that if he sees him as he is being taken up it would be granted; otherwise, it would not. Suddenly chariots of fire and horses of fire appear and pass between them—not separating them as most modern readers assume, but uniting them, not unlike the way the iconostasis serves to unite Orthodox worshipers with what goes on at the altar beyond it. Elisha indicates that he indeed sees what he (along with the reader) is supposed to see, exclaiming "My father, my father, the chariots of Israel and its horsemen!" as his master is taken up in a whirlwind.

Contrary to Jewish and Christian traditions, the fiery chariot does not serve as Elijah's personal conveyance, especially given that Elisha cries out about chariots in the plural both here and later on when he invokes the Lord for a host of them (2 Kings 6). Rather, the exclamation is indicative of something transpiring between them. As he was admonished to do, Elisha *sees* and therefore receives the prophetic inheritance symbolized by the fiery chariots, a literary symbol affirming the line of true biblical prophets as Israel's highest and best line of defense. Once Elijah has been taken up, the illegitimate prophets of the northern shrines organize a search. Elisha discourages them and after three days without success, he retorts, "I told you so!" (v. 18). As in the case of Moses, the author preemptively dismisses out of hand any plans one might have for seeking the graves of the true biblical prophets, lest anyone should miss the point of their lives by seeking to erect a shrine to these bizarre men of God. We see from the Elijah/Elisha cycle that the prophet's mission is never accomplished until God deems it to be so. Even when the prophet's body is all used up and ushered out of view, his life and death cry out, "This was never about me!"

The story of the Man of God (*ish ha-elohim*) from Judah, in 1 Kings 13, offers a textbook example showcasing biblical prophecy's collective ego check and illustrates the prophetic distinction between medium and message. Clearly, the story has developed in two stages. In the first part, an itinerant prophet clearly fitting the Deuteronomistic job description outlined in Deut 9:22 and 13:2-6, foretells the destruction of Jeroboam's altar by the future king Josiah. The second part, in which the man of God is tricked into dining with yet another one of those annoying prophets of Bethel, appears to have been added later, significantly reworking the story into a kind of riddle into the nature of what constitutes a true biblical prophet. Although the Man of God was deceived into disobeying the divine command not to eat or drink during the course of his mission, God kills him and places a lion alongside him to guard his body even though his words to the king are demonstrably true.

This story serves as an effective and enjoyable classroom exercise that requires students to think critically about the real nature of biblical prophecy. This puzzling story requires them to struggle with the question of whether or not the Man of God should be considered a true biblical prophet, a question not so easily answered on its face. On the one hand, the actions of the Man of God achieve the divine will of informing King Jeroboam of things to come, but on the other hand as a man the Man of God is shown to be fallibly human in transgressing God's command and suffering the punishment of death. But just as in the case of the Elijah/Elisha cycle's divinely-ordained regime changes, the historical objective was accomplished irrespective of the personal identities of the agents involved. Here again our prophetical writer seems to be affirming that true prophetic activities and their earthly results have nothing to do with the person of the prophet at all.

Prophetic Self-Negation in the Latter Prophets

The book of Jonah offers one of the best examples of the principle of prophetic self-negation. It relates the story of a prophet who flees his assigned mission because he is unable to grasp the fact that God's salvific activity in the world is universal and independent of what he thinks. Although the book of Jonah is included in the Book of the Twelve, ironically, one finds no direct prophetic message within it. It is clearly fictional, given Jonah's three-day survival in the belly of a great fish (not a whale!), and given its notable regard for the animals of Nineveh reads almost like a fable. How does one make sense of the fact that this book, so different from the rest of the prophetic books on the scroll, sits among them?

Certainly, the tale is more folkloric than oracular, but its inclusion is no doubt purposeful. As I have suggested elsewhere, the tale is right at home among the Prophets and that it simply needs to be understood "inside out" as a self-directed, literary finger-poke in the eye, a self-deprecating, in-house reminder of the critical need for those who would revere the prophet—or perhaps style themselves to be a prophet—to remain authentic to the responsibility such a role entails.[10] In this sense, Jonah may be viewed as *anti-prophet*, a foil who exceeds even Elijah (1 Kings 19) in terms of his utter failure to persuade the Holy One to ameliorate his own physical and self-righteous moral discomforts and whose ego dares challenge the divine plan.

Alongside other prophetic books proper, Jonah becomes the exception that proves the rule. Its inclusion among the Twelve diffuses any accusation that the prophetic guild may be some cold, dead institution existing for its own sake, a kind of photo negative serving as a foil to the prophets' own tradition that invites thinking about what a prophet is truly all about—perhaps at a time when the legendary prophets of the past represented an all too unreachable standard for an ongoing phenomenon. The story acknowledges that prophets themselves are unique characters—and indeed each one is—however, their character traits are merely ornamental, allowing for a "there/not-there" quality that permits the divine Word to be heard loudly and clearly. Sitting under the gourd tree, Jonah,

---

[10] Nicolae Roddy, "Foreword." *How Jonah is Interpreted in Judaism, Christianity, and Islam.* Mishael M. Caspi and John T. Greene, eds.; Lewiston, NY: Edwin Mellen Press, 2011, i-v.

like the fugitive Elijah, expresses his wish to die in order to be released from the burden of his servitude (a second time, if one counts Jonah's earlier desire to be thrown overboard!). But as it is for Elijah, there is no validation of self-pity, nor any personal protest appeased so long as there are kings to be toppled or Ninevites (and their cattle) to be redeemed.

Prophetic self-negation—the distinction of prophet as human from his or her divine mission—is especially apparent in the rejection of their calling. As with Moses, who offers excuses and kindles divine anger by entreating the Lord to send someone else to confront Pharaoh (Exod 4:14), the latter, so-called "writing" prophets resist their missions or downplay their personal involvements in various ways. Amos confronts Amaziah, Jeroboam II's high priest at Bethel, who tells the prophet to return to Judah and earn his livelihood there, to which Amos replies that he is ". . . not a prophet, nor a prophet's son, but a herdsman and dresser of sycamores." Amos's assertion that he is not a prophet (*lo-nabi anoki*), words echoed in a different context in Zech 13:5, may also be translated "I was not a prophet," which would have to add "before now" since he behaves as one. Another possibility is that Amos is asserting he does not belong to the official guild of prophets associated with the state-supporting cult established by Jeroboam and continued generations later by his namesake, Jeroboam II. In any event, the point of Amos's reply to Amaziah remains clear, "Don't make this about me! It is between your king and the Almighty."

Jeremiah offers excuses for why he should not be called to prophesy, stating his inability to speak effectively as a youth (Jer 1:6); however, as in the case of Moses God promises to supply him with the words he needs.

Do not say, "I am only a boy,"
for you shall go to all to whom I send you,
and you shall speak whatever I command you.
Do not be afraid of them,

for I am with you to deliver you, says the Lord.
Then the Lord put out his hand and touched my mouth, and the
Lord said to me:
Now I have put my words in your mouth.
See, today I appoint you over nations and over kingdoms,
to pluck up and to pull down,
to destroy and to overthrow,
to build and to plant.

Isaiah, too, is reluctant to be a vessel of the Holy One, who as
Jerusalem's High Priest he experiences in the temple: "Woe is
me! I am lost, for I am a man of unclean lips, and I live among
a people of unclean lips, yet my eyes have seen the King, the
Lord of hosts!" Only after an angelic being touches his lips with
a burning coal from the altar, removing his unworthiness and
giving him the words to speak, can he answer the Lord's call
"Whom shall I send?" with "Here am I; send me!"
(Isa 6:5-8).

Ezekiel, another Jerusalem priest called to prophesy, does not
overtly express reluctance to fulfill his mission, but God's
concerns for fear and resistance on the part of the prophet
suggest a distinction between the man and the message, which
as in the cases of Moses and Isaiah require the infusion of the
word they must deliver:

> And you, mortal, do not be afraid of them and do not be afraid
> of their words, although rebellious deniers surround you and you
> live among scorpions; do not be afraid of their words nor
> dismayed by their looks, for they are a rebellious house. And you
> shall speak my words unto them, whether they hear or refuse to
> hear, for they are rebellious. But you, mortal, hear what I say to
> you; do not be rebellious like that rebellious house; open your
> mouth and eat what I give you.

> I looked and saw a hand outstretched and holding a scroll. He
> spread it before me; it had writing on the front and on the back
> and written on it were words of lamentation and mourning and
> woe. (Ezek 2:6-10)

Even after the prophet is equipped with the divine word, the distinction between the man and the message remains apparent, as in the case of Jeremiah, whose struggle with the message he bears persists:

> I have become a laughingstock all the day;
> everyone mocks me.
> For whenever I speak, I must cry out;
> I must shout, "Violence and destruction!"
> For the word of the Lord has become for me
> a reproach and derision all day long.
> If I say, "I will not mention him
> or speak any more in his name,"
> then within me there is something like a burning fire
> shut up in my bones;
> I am weary with holding it in,
> but I cannot.
>
> [. . .]
>
> Cursed be the day
> on which I was born!
> The day when my mother bore me,
> let it not be blessed!
> Cursed be the man
> who brought the news to my father, saying,
> "A child is born to you, a son,"
> making him very glad.
> Let that man be like the cities
> that the Lord overthrew without pity;
> let him hear a cry in the morning
> and an alarm at noon,
> because he did not kill me in the womb;
> so my mother would have been my grave
> and her womb forever pregnant.
> Why did I come forth from the womb
> to see toil and sorrow
> and spend my days in shame? (Jer 20:7b-14)

In the end, what binds the prophets together is the apparent self-awareness that the Word must be heard and taken seriously, irrespective of their own human limitations. The prophet functions as a true religious symbol in that he (less often, she) participates in the realm of the Sacred while remaining flawed and fully human. Whether it is Isaiah walking naked and unshod through the streets of Jerusalem (Isa 20:2-4); Jeremiah removing his soiled, tattered underwear from the cleft of a rock and waving it in the face of the people (Jer 13:1-11); Ezekiel becoming a bizarre spectacle or scandalizing the community by ignoring public mourning rituals upon the death of his wife; such scenarios ultimately draw attention *through* the medium to the Source beyond, bringing a society of transgressors face to face with the living God. The danger for the prophetic tradition would lie in taking itself too seriously, becoming a cult of personality and neglecting the responsibility for which it has been called. For the prophetic tradition, what it means *ultimately* to be human is to act with an eye toward transcending the ego self and acting for the greater good, even at great personal expense. One sees that the commandment "You shall have no other gods before me" (Exod 20:3 / Deut 5:7) applies as much to the exercise of one's own individual self as it does to the veneration of idols of inert wood and stone.

Conclusion: Prophetic Self-Negation as Paradigm

Prophetic self-negation offers an effective model for countering many of the ills that plague modern society, especially problems of angst and despair among our younger generations. Giving oneself over to social media and what others think is like living in slavery in Pharaoh's Egypt, in complete denial of what it means to be a human being bound to the scriptural God. How the prophetic model of self-negation challenges the ills of contemporary society will be addressed in the final chapter, which deals with the building blocks of idolatrous society, namely, the ego self.

Chapter 8
The Trouble with Self

"I Am that I Am." (Exod 3:14)

"You shall have no other gods before me." (Exod 20:3)

As we have seen, the prophetically influenced priestly scribal critique of human endeavors is directed not so much at the institutions themselves but at human attitudes towards them. For all recorded history, human beings have trusted in the works of their hands for safety and security, all the while paying lip service to their respective gods. The book of Judges presents an ongoing cycle of the Israelites' "forgetting" the Lord God of their deliverance who jars them into remembrance by raising up an enemy against them. For a brief time, they rid themselves of idolatry only to return to the habits of mindlessness and self-delusion to which they were accustomed.

Levantine societies in antiquity were characterized by varying circles of relationship, moving outward from family and extended family toward more removed degrees of interaction and trust to clan, tribe, and people (ethnos). The health of any social organism depends on cooperation among persons in a way that balances personal needs with those of their society so that both may thrive. Still, as living organisms, societies eventually die away. Governments fail, cities collapse, weapons bring destruction, money flows to corrupt elites, temples become vain monuments, and self-proclaimed prophets lead people to an unhappy end. This is how the answer to the question of "What went wrong?" so occupied the minds of the prophetically influenced priestly scribes who stood dazed and confused at the smoldering end of their national history. Their answer to the question was a collective "We did!" The pride and arrogance of their nation—and every nation, each with its own tower of Babel—arose from idolatry, that is, forgetting the Lord and trusting in the works of their own hands. However, the foundational predicament remains a particularly singular one, for systemic social dis-ease is ultimately rooted in the problem of the ego. When the idol of Self is worshipped and glorified, any action, no matter how despicable, becomes self-justifiable. If the idol of Self is recognized for the idol it is and toppled, other idols are easily cast down.

One can imagine that the process of considering the true self begins with the open question expressed by the Psalmist:

> When I look at the heavens, the works of your fingers, the moon and the stars you have established, what are human beings [*ma enosh?*] that you are mindful of them, and mortals that you attend them? (Ps 8:4-5)

Whatever the answer, the question arises within the context of creation:

> Then God said, "Let us make humankind (*'adam*) in our image (*tselem*), according to our likeness (*demuth*); and let them rule (*radah*) over the fish of the sea, and over the birds of the air, and over the livestock, and over all the earth, and over every creeping thing that creeps upon the earth." So God created humankind in his own image, in the image of God he created them; male and female he created them. And God blessed them and said to them, "Be fruitful and multiply and fill the earth and subdue it . . ." (Gen 1:26-28a)

Here a problem arises in the traditional interpretation of "image and likeness" (*tselem ve-demuth*, cf. Gen 1:26-27; 5:1-2; 9:6; cf. Ps 17:15; Eccl 7:20), a topic so pervasive in biblical and theological literature that it challenges credulity to imagine anything more could be said on the subject.[1] In fact, the last

---

[1] In an article written well over four decades ago, J. Maxwell Miller observes the fact that biblical scholars had already so thoroughly exhausted the topic of the Priestly writer's use of the terms *image* (*tselem*) and *likeness* (*demuth*) that "one may question whether any further significant observations can possibly be made." J. Maxwell Miller, "In the 'Image' and 'Likeness' of God," *JBL* 91.3 (1972), 289–304 (289). Of course, in the New Testament the image of God is fulfilled in Christ, in whom "all the fullness of God was pleased to dwell" (Col 1:15, 19; cf. 2 Cor 4:4), but that would be another volume.

several decades have witnessed tiresome reiteration of the same basic points:

- The writer's usage of *image* and *likeness* is unique, but these concepts are known throughout the ancient Near East;[2]

- As an example of Hebrew parallelism, the terms are practically synonymous;[3]

- They distinguish human beings—male and female—from the rest of creation, indicating that humans are related to the Creator in some special way;[4]

- They are couched in royal language (*radah*, to rule, have dominion) that seems to elevate human beings to a status reserved in the ancient Near East only for royalty.[5]

Source critical considerations have led writers to speculate how these sparse details might address the whole of the human person, resulting in creative and open-ended ideas for human *being* vis-à-vis the Deity, with one another, with the environment, or with oneself. But apart from being created male and female, commissioned to have "dominion" over creation, and commanded to propagate it is not at all clear what being created in God's image and likeness really entails, opening the door for interpreters to fashion human beings in their own privileged images and likenesses. In the end, Genesis 1 is insufficient for discovering any complete picture of biblical

---

[2] James Barr, "The Image of God in the Book of Genesis—A Study of Terminology," *Bulletin of the John Rylands Library* 51.1 (1968), 11-26.

[3] Ibid., 24-25.

[4] W. Randall Garr, *In His Own Image and Likeness: Humanity, Divinity, and Monotheism* (Leiden: Brill, 2003). On matters of gender in Gen 3:26-27, see Phyllis Trible, *God and the Rhetoric of Sexuality* (Philadelphia: Fortress, 1978), 12-21.

[5] See J. Richard Middleton, *The Liberating Image: The Imago Dei in Genesis I* (Grand Rapids, MI: Brazos, 2005), 15-29.

anthropology; one must consider the entirety of scripture.[6] Of course, for Orthodox Christians, the image of God is fulfilled in Jesus Christ, but what sort of model does that entail? Clearly a mistake is made when we make this cosmogony all about humans. If the priestly writer had in mind to address the subject of theological anthropology, no doubt he would have been much clearer about it. With so little insight provided within the chapter itself, we must seek an intertextual solution—one that includes the prophetic perspective.

The prophetic starting point for exploring what it might mean to be created in the image and likeness of God begins with biblical descriptions of the scriptural God. A comprehensive review of prophetic literature reveals the most oft-used metaphor for God is "King" (*melek*):

> Thus says the Lord, the King of Israel, and his Redeemer, the Lord of hosts: I am the first, and I am the last; besides me there is no God. (Isa 44:6)

> The Lord reigns; let all nations tremble! He sits enthroned upon the cherubim; let the earth quake. (Ps 99:1)

In places where the term *melek* is not explicitly used, it is implied in royal language associated with ruling and enthronement (e.g., 1 Sam 4:4; 2 Sam 6:2; 2 Kgs 19:15; Isa 33:22, 37:16, 40:22; 1 Chr 13:6, 29:12; Ps 80:2, 103:19). While the title is all but absent in the Torah, it is implied in the story of the Exodus, in which Yahweh delivers the Hebrews from servitude and binds them to himself in a covenant relationship requiring obedience to the divine law.

Still, the picture of God as King does not say much about what it means for humans to be created in the image and likeness of God. We must turn to prophetic literature and the Psalms to find another significant descriptor, that of the shepherd (*ro'eh*):

---

[6] Robert Briggs, "Humans in the Image of God and Other Things Genesis Does Not Make Clear," *Journal of Theological Interpretation* 4.1 (2010), 111-126 (112).

> As a shepherd looks out for his flock when he is among the scattered sheep, so will I seek out my sheep and deliver them from all the places to which they have been scattered on the day of clouds and thick darkness (Ezek 34:12)

> The Lord is my shepherd (Ps 23:1)

> Give ear, O Shepherd of Israel, you who lead Joseph like a flock (80:1)

Understanding the God of Scripture as Shepherd and King does not ensure earthly kings will lead and shepherd their people, for as we saw in Chapter Two, human kings usually behave as gods themselves—self-serving at best; ruthless despots at worst—with truly benevolent kings the stuff of wishful legend.

> O mortal, prophesy against the shepherds of Israel, prophesy and say to them, even to the shepherds, "Thus says the Lord God: Woe unto the shepherds of Israel that have fed themselves. Should not the shepherds feed their sheep? (Ezek 34:2)

Whereas biblical kings, including the once-shepherd David, behave as self-serving autocrats, God as Shepherd and King manifests absolute sovereignty in the universe while protecting the ultimate well-being of the flock through the strict demand of unwavering obedience necessary for its survival: "Walk in the way I command you, that it may be well with you" (Jer 7:23). Thus, fulfilling the image and likeness of God does not permit one to act uniquely as a god, but requires strict obedience to the responsibility of ensuring the well-being of those within one's charge who belong to God. At the end of the day, the flipside to God's self-revelation as the great "I Am" (Exod 3:14) is a resolute "You're not!" This obligation to extend the sovereignty of God, as opposed to manufacturing one's own brand of it, not only applies to kings and political leaders, but also to parents and teachers, older brothers and sisters, employers and coaches, and so on.

Next, it is important to explore the motive that underlies this human responsibility to others. Looking again to Scripture, the motivation for God's meaningful action in the cosmos is *hesed* (Gr. *agape*), often translated as steadfast lovingkindness. In Psalm 136, it appears no less than twenty-six times, where it is usually translated as "mercy." Such ubiquitous use of the term indicates unfailing love on the part of the Shepherd and King: "Although the mountains pass away and the hills disappear, my steadfast love for you will not depart from you" (Isa 54:10). *Hesed*, in contrast to modern ideas of love, does not involve some intense emotional feeling, but rather action carried out for the benefit of others, perhaps to feed, clothe, or defend from danger or injustice.

Looking to the scriptural Shepherd and King, we see *hesed* manifested throughout the cosmos by means of the twinned attributes of justice and righteousness (*mishpat ve-tzedakah*). The word translated "justice," *mishpat*, has as its root the Hebrew verb *sh-p-t*, which can mean "to rule," "to warn," "to judge," or "to punish." The substantive form can mean "justice," "judgment," "vindication," and more, depending on context. The word *tzedakah* is equally ambiguous and is sometimes used synonymously with *mishpat*, but by translating it as "righteousness" in contrast with *mishpat* (as in the biblical text) the shades of meaning serve a significant function here. When these words are paired, as they so often are throughout the prophets (especially in Isaiah) they form a kind of synonymous parallelism or hendiadys, a pairing of nouns that opens a semantic range beyond anything the terms would convey independently on their own. Justice derives from the principle of equality, a property that human beings have a natural ability to recognize, while righteousness refers to the way things should be from a scriptural perspective.

The pairing of these terms serves as the most oft-used attribute of the scriptural God. As Shepherd and King of all creation, the supreme Judge of the world establishes the only legitimate standard of justice by bringing the possibility of righteousness to fruition among all peoples:

> The Lord is King; let the peoples tremble!
> He sits enthroned upon the cherubim; let the earth quake!
> The Lord is great in Zion; he is exalted over all peoples.
> Let all peoples praise Your great and awesome name. Holy is he!
> Mighty king, lover of justice, you have established equity;
> You have executed justice and righteousness in Jacob.
> Extol the Lord our God; worship at his footstool. Holy is he!
> (Ps 99:1-5)

Psalm 97 also associates justice and righteousness with God's sovereign majesty:

> The Lord is king! Let the earth rejoice;
> let the many coastlands be glad!
> Clouds and thick darkness are all around him;
> righteousness and justice are the foundation of his throne.
> (vv. 1-2)

The connection between justice and righteousness is strengthened in their reciprocity as divine attributes. Ps 9:8 proclaims that God "judges the world with righteousness," while elsewhere, "You are righteous O Lord, and your judgments are right" (Ps 119:137). According to Jeremiah's scribe, these twinned divine attributes are not to be ignored by those who hold power and authority over others:

> Thus says the Lord: Do not let the wise boast in their wisdom, do not let the mighty boast in their might, do not let the wealthy boast in their wealth; but let those who boast do so in this, that they understand and know me, that I am the Lord; I act with steadfast love (*hesed*), justice, and righteousness in the earth; for in these things I delight, says the Lord. (Jer 9:23-24)

Such will be the way of Jeremiah's "righteous branch" from the house of David, who shall reign as king and deal wisely, and shall execute justice and righteousness in the land."

> The days are surely coming, says the Lord, when I will raise up for David a righteous Branch, and he shall raise as king and deal wisely, and shall execute justice and righteousness in the land. In his days Judah will be saved and Israel will live in safety. And this

is the name by which he will be called: "The Lord is our righteousness." (Jer 23:5-6)

Jeremiah's witness to the fact that the handing down of justice and righteousness is lacking among Jerusalem's leaders finds remedy in the Psalms:

Give the king your justice, O God,
and your righteousness to a king's son.
May he judge your people with righteousness,
and your poor with justice. (Ps 72:1-2)
God has taken his place in the divine council;
in the midst of the gods, he holds judgment:
"How long will you judge unjustly
and show partiality to the wicked?
Give justice to the weak and the orphan;
maintain the right of the lowly and the destitute.
Rescue the weak and the needy;
deliver them from the hand of the wicked. (Ps 82:1-4)

Finally, nowhere is the proverb, "To do righteousness and justice is more acceptable to the Lord than sacrifice" (Prov 21:3) better illustrated than in this oft-quoted passage in Amos, which voices God's disdain for the empty offerings of animal and song in a land where justice and righteousness are lacking. The execution of justice and righteousness are far more important than cultic piety. Care for the disadvantaged righteous poor (Ps 10:17-18) must take place for ritual sacrifice to become acceptable to God:

I hate, I despise your festivals,
and I take no delight in your solemn assemblies.
Even though you offer me your burnt offerings and grain offerings,
I will not accept them;
and the offerings of well-being of your fatted animals
I will not look upon.
Take away from me the noise of your songs;
I will not listen to the melody of your harps.
But let justice roll down like waters,
and righteousness like an ever-flowing stream. (Amos 5:21-24)

In sum, the pairing of justice and righteousness is therefore of paramount importance for the question of what it means to be created in the image and likeness of God. Although the terms are ascribed to the Shepherd and King, and expected of humans (e.g., Amos 5:24), their contrasting shades of meaning combine to form two sides of the same coin, which must be held in balance; for on the one hand righteousness without justice in regard to the critical appraisal of self easily results in self-righteousness and self-justification. On the other hand, the execution of justice without righteousness can lead to a lack of mercy toward oneself and others. The first of these imbalances—self-righteousness—is seen in the attitudes of Job (Job 32:1) and the prophet Jonah, while the latter imbalance is illustrated by David's abuse of *mishpat* in light of Uriah's unswerving loyalty to his fellows (2 Samuel 11).

Consciously or not, human beings stand at the center of three concentric circles of justice commensurate with degrees of scriptural righteousness. The closest circle involves perceived injustice to oneself that, real or imagined, human beings are very quick to recognize, usually in the form of suffering, despair, or reacting out of indignity and pain. This circle does not entail a great deal of righteousness. The second circle, which must often be called to our awareness, involves perceived injustice to those with whom one is acquainted and for whom one is likely to feel some degree of sympathy. This is the beginning of scriptural righteousness. The third and outermost circle—and the most difficult—involves injustice suffered by people we do not know or may not even like. This includes taking actions on behalf of the poor and homeless dwelling within our own neighborhoods, to those dying of famine or languishing unjustly in prisons here and abroad. This is full righteousness, the true *hesed*. "This is my commandment, that you love one another as I have loved you" (Jn 15:12). The third circle necessarily involves righteousness in that one must go beyond the self to make it operational, not averting the eyes when it would be easier to do so.

The Garden of Eden story (Gen 2:4b–3:24) offers further insight into the role of human beings in creation. The traditional interpretation takes the woman at her word that the serpent tricked her into disobedience; however, the serpent's words reflect the fact that the only difference between gods and humans in antiquity was that gods possess special knowledge and live forever. The woman sees that the tree is beautiful to behold, good for food, and desirable for attaining wisdom (Gen 3:6), so as long as the humans have access to both trees, they would indeed be "as gods," or "like God" (*Elohim*, a plural form). Thus, the expulsion from Eden appears to be an effort on the part of Yahweh (more precisely, the writer) to preserve the uniqueness of the Supreme Being, who has given humans right of access to either one tree or the other, but not to both. This interpretation is confirmed by the end of the third chapter:

> Then the Lord God said, "See, the humans have become like one of us, knowing good and evil—and now they might reach out their hands and take also from the tree of life and eat and live forever." Therefore, the Lord God sent them forth from the garden of Eden to till the ground from which they were taken. He drove out the humans, and at the east of the garden of Eden he placed the cherubim and a flaming sword turning this way and that to guard the way to the tree of life. (Gen 3:22-24)

The motif of humans desiring to be as gods (or like God, since Elohim is a plurality) appears again in the Babel story as humans conspire to build a tower extending to the world's upper tier, the realm of the divine that is forbidden to them. Yahweh, of course, does not permit such trespass. Human plans are thwarted; their languages are confused, and their tribes are scattered over the face of the earth. Aspiring to be as gods, they must be returned to their rightful place in the three-tiered world.

The distinction between the divine and human is further reinforced in the book of Exodus, where Moses encounters an angel of the Lord in a burning bush while tending the flock of his father-in-law Jethro near Mt. Horeb (Exod 3:1-12).

Responding to the question of who is commissioning him to go to Egypt to liberate his fellow Hebrews, the voice of God replies, "I am who I am; thus, you shall say to the Israelites, 'I Am has sent me to you.'" The writer's identification of God in the self-defining singular, "I Am who I am" (or "I will be Who I will be") further supports the uniqueness of God, as well the implication "You're not."

Conclusion

Personal desire, especially the need to acquire and control persons and things, is the fundamental human predicament leading to suffering and despair.[7] The underlying desire to acquire and control arises from the imperceptible reality of personal fear and insecurity in the world; thus, those among us who attempt to exercise the most control over persons and things tend to be the most fearful and insecure. Reliance upon strong man-type leaders, personal wealth, material defenses, and so on creates an illusory veil of security that when pulled away leaves the fearful and insecure unprepared for the ultimate reality that lies beyond the veneer of self-deception. These idolatrous personal proclivities contribute to an overall idolatrous society, which in turn only reinforces the personal pathology that prevents one from being truly free in obedience to the law of Scripture.

---

[7] This statement finds agreement in the first and second predicates of Buddhism's Four Noble Truths, namely that all beings suffer, and that suffering is caused by desire.

Select Bibliography

Brett, Mark G. *Biblical Criticism in Crisis? The Impact of the Canonical Approach on Old Testament Studies*. Cambridge: Cambridge University Press, 1991.

Brettler, Marc. "The Copenhagen School: The Methodological Issues," *AJS Review* 27:1 (2003): 1-22.

Childs, Brevard. *Introduction to the Old Testament as Scripture*. Philadelphia: Fortress Press, 1979.

Cross, Frank M. "The Structure of the Deuteronomistic History," in *Perspectives in Jewish Learning*, edited by J. M. Rosenthal, 9-24. ACJS 3; Chicago: College of Jewish Studies, 1968.

_____. *Canaanite Myth and Hebrew Epic: Essays in the History of the Religion* of Israel; Cambridge: Harvard University Press, 1973.

Davies, Philip. *In Search of "Ancient Israel."* JSOTSup 148; Sheffield: JSOT Press, 1992.

Dozeman, Thomas. B, Thomas Römer, and Konrad Schmid, *Pentateuch, Hexateuch, or Enneateuch?: Identifying Literary Works in Genesis through Kings*. Atlanta: Society of Biblical Literature, 2011.

Grabbe, Lester, ed. *Can a History of Israel Be Written?* JSOTSup 245; Sheffield: Sheffield Academic Press, 1997.

Finkelstein, Israel, and Neil Asher Silberman. *The Bible Unearthed: Archaeology's New Vision of Ancient Israel and the Origin of Its Sacred Texts*. New York: Touchstone, 2002.

Lemche, Neils Peter. *Early Israel: Anthropological and Historical Studies on the Israelite Society Before the Monarchy*. VTSup 37; Leiden: E. J. Brill, 1985.

_____. "The Old Testament—a Hellenistic Book?" *SJOT* 7 (1993): 163-93.

Nadav, Na'aman, "Was Khirbet Qeiyafa a Judahite City? The Case Against It," *JHS* 17.7 (2017). doi:10.5508/jhs.2017.v17.a7.

Noth, Martin. *Überlieferungsgeschichte des Pentateuch*. Stuttgart: Kohlhammer, 1948; reprinted: *A History of Pentateuchal Traditions*. Englewood Cliffs, NJ: Prentice-Hall, 1972.

Rendtorff, Rolf. *Canon and Theology*. Minneapolis: Fortress Press, 1993.

Tarazi, Paul Nadim. *The Rise of Scripture*. St. Paul, MN: OCABS Press, 2017.

_____. *Decoding Genesis 1–11*. St. Paul, MN: OCABS Press, 2020.

Thompson, Thomas L. *The Historicity of the Patriarchal Narratives*. BZAW 133; Berlin: de Gruyter, 1974.

_____. *Early History of the Israelite People from the Written and Archaeological Sources*. SHANE 4; Leiden: Brill, 1992.

Van Seeters, John. *Abraham in History and Tradition*. New Haven: Yale University Press, 1975.

About the Author

Nicolae Roddy is a Romanian-American Orthodox professor of Hebrew Bible/Older Testament at Creighton University, a leading four-year Jesuit Catholic Liberal Arts institution located in Omaha, Nebraska, where he has taught for the past quarter century. Since 2003, Roddy has served as Faculty Associate and Visiting Professor for the Hebraic Studies Center at the University of Bucharest. For twenty years, he co-directed and supervised the Bethsaida Archaeology Project, located at the foot of the Golan Heights near the northwestern shore of the Sea of Galilee. A Fulbright scholar, Roddy conducted research in Romania during the 1994-1995 academic year, which led to the publication of *The Romanian Version of the Testament of Abraham: Text, Translation, and Cultural Context* (Atlanta, GA: Society of Biblical Literature, 2001). He has since produced other volumes and dozens of peer-reviewed articles. Roddy is married to Alexandra, formerly of Bucharest, and is the father of five remarkable children.

9 781601 910578